widows gone wild

OUR JOURNEY FROM LOSS TO RESILIENCE

SUNNY WELLS

RETELLING, LLC

Copyright © 2019 by Gladys Wells

All rights reserved.
ISBN-13: 978-1-7336296-0-7

Published by Retelling | retelling.net

Cover design by Cynthia Young | youngdesign.biz
Cover photo by Wattanapong plymat/iStock

*"In everyone's life, at some time, our inner fire goes out.
It is then burst into flame by an encounter
with another human being.
We should all be thankful for those people
who rekindle the inner spirit."*

ALBERT SCHWEITZER, DOCTOR AND PHILOSOPHER

---

*Rhonda, Janet, Mary, Debbie, Jan, Sue, Karen ...
We met in a way that no one would ever wish for,
but our bond is stronger than any I have experienced.
You truly helped me to rekindle my inner spirit.*

SUNNY

Dedicated to the memory of Terry Kruschwitz

CONTENTS

INTRODUCTION. . . . . *vii*

1. All Too Soon 1
2. Ready to Go. 5
3. Saying Goodbye. 13
4. Which is Harder? 17
5. Last Visits 29
6. Where Did You Go? 33
7. Am I Crazy? 37
8. Magical Thinking. 43
9. Missing the Deceased 47
10. Place to Remember 51
11. Guilty Relief 55
12. New Life Strategies 59
13. Value of Group 63
14. Jolly Group 69
15. The Power of Listening. 71
16. 911/411. 77
17. Letting Go 81
18. Taking Off the Ring 89
19. Moving Forward 93
20. Widows Gone Wild 99
21. Reinvesting in Life 107
22. Time Does Heal, with Help . . 111
23. A New Way to Mark Time . . . 115
24. Keeping Traditions Alive 121

25. Sacred Space............. 125
26. Patterns of Resilience....... 129
27. Not Replacing Anybody 133
28. New Life, Old Fear 139
29. All Will Be Well........... 141

ACKNOWLEDGEMENTS .. 147
REFERENCES 149
ABOUT THE AUTHOR ... 151

INTRODUCTION

When Joe Biden was comforting the family of John McCain at McCain's memorial service in August 2018, he said,

> "But I make you a promise. I promise you, the time will come that what's going to happen is six months will go by and everybody is going to think, well, it's passed. But you are going to ride by that field or smell that fragrance or see that flashing image. You are going to feel like you did the day you got the news. But you know you are going to make it. The image of your dad, your husband, your friend. It crosses your mind and a smile comes to your lips before a tear to your eye. That's [how] you know. I promise you, I give you my word, I promise you, this I know. The day will come. That day will come."

As I listened to those words, I nodded my head with tears in my eyes. I remembered those months after my husband Terry died when I couldn't imagine life ever going back to me caring about and enjoying everyday things again. As the weeks and months passed, and the members of the Younger Bereaved Spouses support group marked the anniversary dates of our loved ones' passings (one month, six months, one year), one truth stood out for me: *I would not have made it this far this soon without the support of people who had been through the same thing.* The difference in healing for me between doing it on your own or being in a group was that whenever I felt like I was alone in my struggle, or that I was probably going crazy, talking about it in the group helped me realize I was not alone, and others were having the same crazy thoughts.

I am forever grateful that one gloomy April evening, I decided to leave the safety and loneliness of my home and venture out to that life-changing place.

Now that I am on "the other side of sadness," one of the purposes in my life is to help other people in their grief. When I hear of someone who has just lost a spouse, at any age, I can literally feel his or her pain. I hope the story of my loss and my journey to resilience, along with the Widows Gone Wild, will help in at least some small way. I want you to know that you are not alone, that your grief, though unique to you, has been experienced by many people before you. You will get through this and come out stronger on the other side. This book will help you see that is entirely possible. I wish you peace in your journey.

· I ·
ALL TOO SOON

ON A WET SPRING DAY in late April, about a month after Terry had died, I parked my car on Cherry Street and sat for a moment, gazing up at the building beside me. After a few moments, I took a deep breath, and slowly climbed out of the car. I rode the elevator up to the seventh floor and entered the meeting room where I found several women and a few men, all close to my age, milling around. I had heard about the Younger Bereaved Spouses support group through Denver Hospice, whose services we had used in the last months of Terry's life.

When I entered the room that evening, I was nervous and didn't know what to expect. I was really just beginning my widowhood journey. During my husband's two-year battle with pancreatic cancer, I had gone through a lot of anticipatory grieving, but now I was officially a full-fledged, real-life widow. I knew I needed some support that my friends and family could not give. It had to come from people who were confronting the same issues as I was: How to survive in a world in which I am no longer part of a couple.

A long table filled the middle of the room, with a candle and sheet of paper at each place. As the approximately twenty of us took our seats, we were asked to go around the table and introduce ourselves.

I'm Sunny, and my husband, Terry, died on March 17 of pancreatic cancer.

I'm Rhonda, and my husband, Mike, died in January 2007 of pancreatic cancer.

I'm Janet, and my husband, Dave, died in January 2007 from fibrosarcoma.

I'm Deb, and my husband, Brant, died in January 2007 of melanoma.

I'm Mary, and my husband, Dan, died in December 2007 of a heart attack.

I'm Sue, and my husband, John, died in September 2006 of thyroid cancer.

And on and on. Eyes were moist, tears rolled down faces.

As I listened to the other young grieving spouses around the table, I pondered the unique aspect of this group's grief: We had all lost a spouse at an earlier age than most people expect. We would never celebrate those big anniversary milestones of 40 years, 50 years or more. Many would never have the joy of sharing with their spouse their children's graduations, weddings, and first grandchildren.

We had each experienced what "until death do us part" felt like. All too soon.

I joined this hospice support group in 2008. Eleven years later (and counting), eight of us still meet regularly and have developed a bond that cannot be broken. Each of us has her own story, but our togetherness has produced individual strength that we hadn't expected. Our little band of survivors matured into the Widows Gone Wild, a circle of friends who helped me work through my grief and develop a resilience I'd never known.

Resilience.

There is no other word to describe it. You either lie down and bury yourself with your lost loved one, or you pick yourself up, put one foot in front of the other and honor that person's memory by living your life in a fashion he would be relieved to see you doing.

. 2 .
READY TO GO

My husband rustled the paper on the clinic table and cleared his throat. I shifted in my seat in the examination room where I had spent many hours in the past two years. Dr. Diab had some news for us, which he delivered in the same gentle manner we had become accustomed to.

I had to be careful with my reactions. A month previous, when we were discussing further treatment options, the doctor asked Terry about his quality of life. My stoic husband replied, "Well, I think I am doing fine." I sat, stunned at these words coming from a man who was by that point usually sitting, head bowed, doubled over in pain even with the strong medications he was taking. It was just another example of how Terry was dealing with his reality. Without thinking, I blurted, "Oh Terry, you are *not* doing well. You are so much worse." He looked at the doctor and in a serious tone said, "She is just trying to pull the plug on me." I was overcome. Even as the doctor was saying, "Terry, you know that is not true," and "This woman has not left your side in all these months," I fled the room. I ducked into a storage closet and cried. Dr. Diab came to find me, explaining this was not all that unusual for someone like Terry who had such a strong will to live. He urged me to return to the room, which I did. Terry and I never spoke about that moment, and I never again gave my unsolicited opinion on treatment options.

And then came this fateful day. Together we listened. The latest tests had come back from my husband's recent PET scan. The oncologist with whom we had developed a special relationship in the past two years said tenderly, "Terry, you have been such a fighter. There is nothing more that can be done."

Terry leaned over the exam table with a familiar gesture he always used with his arms to show that he did not agree, and pleaded, "Isn't there just one more drug that could buy me another month?"

Two of our children were expecting babies that spring. We already had twin granddaughters, whom Terry was very close to, and he couldn't wait for the next two grandchildren. The anticipation of their arrival was one of the motivating factors keeping him alive.

When the doctor assured him there were no other drugs, this emaciated, formerly big, strong man put up his arms in surrender and murmured, "I'm ready to go."

That sentence held so much meaning for me. As I looked at Dr. Diab, we both were aware that Terry was not only ready to go home that day, but he was ready to go to that place where there would be no more struggle.

It was one of the saddest days of my life, even sadder than the day he died. It meant the fight was over.

My struggle, however, was just beginning.

My experience with the Denver Hospice during Terry's last days contributed greatly to my peace of mind and that of my family. The nurses, social workers, and caretakers were kind, helpful, and they gently guided me to the next steps to make Terry comfortable. Once Terry agreed to allow this service to come into our home, my life became more manageable. My only regret was that he did not allow it sooner. To him, it was a step in affirming his mortality. He did not think he needed it, but he finally gave into my assertion that *I* needed it.

After Terry died, the hospice continued to stay in my life, sending me condolences and updates on their services. They had a monthly newsletter with topics relating to what I had just experienced. In one article, there was a description of their support groups. They were loss-specific, and the one that caught my eye was Younger Bereaved Spouses. The group met on the first and third Wednesdays of every month. To join this group, you had to be 59 years of age or younger.

I did not wait long to go to my first meeting. Many of the group were surprised I was attending only a month after my loss. I just knew I needed some support and after my time spent with the Denver Hospice, I felt I could trust them. To be sure, my grief was more raw than the others, and thinking back, I might have waited a bit. Several of the members said later that they attended individual counseling sessions before being brave enough to go to a group. I think my years of caretaking and feeling so isolated contributed to my need to talk about the experience with people who had been through similar losses. I don't discount my loyal friends and family who were there for me before, during, and after Terry's death, but I longed to know if what I was feeling was normal and if there was anything I could do to feel better. And the loss-specific description of Younger Bereaved Spouses spoke to me.

So, one night in early April, less than a month after my loss, I decided to attend. I entered the hospice building, a bit anxious about what I would encounter. Taking the elevator up to the floor where the group was being held, I chatted a bit with another person heading the same way, who assured me I was going to the right place.

When I walked into the room and saw people chatting, I was relieved to see they looked like they enjoyed being there and were not doubled over in grief. I guess I was expecting a more somber, stricken-looking group. The room was beautifully decorated; a long table sat in the middle with comfortable chairs around it. (I had been envisioning a stark, gray room with metal folding chairs). You could see the Rocky Mountains from the room and that somehow gave me strength.

As we took our places, the social worker indicated it was time to begin. She started the group by having us go around and light a candle, telling when our spouses had died and from what causes. We carefully lit our candles, new members of a group none of us wanted to qualify for.

I was surprised this was a helpful exercise for me. It let me know immediately that I was not the only one who had suffered this kind of loss at a younger age. Before that, the term "widow" had conjured up images of old gray-haired women who were going to spend the rest of their lives grieving. The men and women around that table definitely did not fit that description.

I noticed there were fewer men than women around the table. Were there fewer widowers than widows in the world? Are women in our society more willing to share feelings and be more emotionally vulnerable? Are men not encouraged to do so? Perhaps men in our society are more conditioned not to show their emotions. Women are more expected to show emotion and not judged as weak when they do. Probably all of the above, but I can say the men in the Younger Spouses group were feeling the same deep grief and the need to talk about it with those who could relate.

After we finished the candle exercise, the hospice worker, Sarah, told us to take turns reading a list of thoughtful instructions about how to be in a support group. One at a time we read aloud from the papers before us. The hospice center had prepared the inspirational directions to guide us as we started to work through our grief. We each read one of the items on the list aloud.

The instructions guided us to listen, not judge, not give advice, not force anyone to speak who did not want to, and other pointers. Remember why we have come together. Be present as fully as possible. What is offered in the group is by invitation, not demand. Speak your truth in ways that respect another person's truth. No fixing, no saving, no advising, and no setting each other straight. Turn to wonder. Attend to your own inner teacher. Trust and learn from silence. Allow equal time for sharing. Observe deep confidentiality. Know that it's possible to leave the group with whatever it was that you needed when you arrived.

We went around the group one by one until all of the items on the list were read. Softly we read the guidelines and passed the turn to the next person. So many faces. So much pain.

It was then time to talk.

The process flowed smoothly, and even when no one was talking, the silence was not uncomfortable. The faces around that table were so full of empathy and understanding, it was not hard for me to speak. I am by nature a person who will talk about my experiences if I feel anyone wants to listen, and there was no lack of listening around that table.

We took a couple of breaks during the session, and the two hours flew by. A few members of the group came up to me during a break after a particularly heart-wrenching moment. They told me they were sorry and understood.

I had decided to join the group because I needed to talk to someone who would understand. I stayed because it became a safe refuge, a place to say outlandish things and not be judged, a place where I could spend the whole session crying if I needed to and receive comfort.

At that first meeting, Sue, Janet, Rhonda, Deb, and Mary, still complete strangers to me, also sat around that table. Looking back now, I think I felt even a little envious that they were further along than I was in my journey. Jan came later that spring. Karen was an occasional drop-in. I don't think I talked to any of them that first time; it was all I could do to try to contain my emotions a little bit so I wouldn't end up on the floor in a sobbing heap.

Within weeks, I was no longer nervous entering that room; instead a sense of relief flooded over me every time I walked through the door. The recent memories of the darkest days of my life didn't go away overnight. It helped me to be able to express my fresh pain with new friends who shared similar tragedy.

· 3 ·
SAYING GOODBYE

As Terry approached his 55th birthday, he had become so frail, he rarely ventured farther than the kitchen and the bedroom. We finally got a hospice bed delivered to our house, something he had fought for a long time.

One day I asked him, "Terry, would you like a birthday party, an open house where people could come and see you and visit?" He immediately said, "Yes." This was unlike him, as he never wanted attention for himself on days like that.

In a short time, I was able to get a party going. His birthday was March 9, a Sunday in 2008, making it the perfect day for the open house. I quickly sent out emails to neighbors, friends, and co-workers.

Terry was adamant there be "a lot of food and a big cake" at his party. He was always such a foodie, and to him, hospitality meant feeding your friends well. He did that for our kids' weddings too. Terry liked to provide a lot of food. Our son, Joel, related in his eulogy at Terry's funeral about a time he and his dad were talking about funerals. Terry had said, "Man, I just love food at funerals. I mean, of course you miss the person who is no longer there, but the food everybody brings is so good!"

After Terry expressed his desire to look good for the party, the hospice nurse brought over a volunteer who shaved him and cut his hair.

The morning of Terry's birthday, we all went to Mass, something he hadn't been able to do for quite some time. After Mass, we got Terry home and settled in his chair. When I returned from the store with the pre-ordered food and cake, Terry insisted I stop at his chair and show him everything on the trays. He wanted to see every tray, get a close up look at the cake, and double check that there was enough beer. He told me what a great job I had done planning his party. He was very happy.

"Terry, would you like me to fix you a plate?" He said yes, and even though I knew he would not be able to eat a thing, I fixed a plate with one of everything on it.

"And a beer," he requested weakly. He was going to enjoy that birthday.

The plate remained on his tray the entire afternoon. He was able to eat a bite of cake (always his favorite), and drink a sip or two of beer, but nothing else.

About sixty people came and went during that difficult afternoon. I could tell when people entered the living room they were shocked to see this formerly big strapping man sitting in that chair, looking like he was 90. Guests milled around, trying to look normal.

He was able to sit up in his chair and visit, recounting old stories with friends. I have a photo of Terry from behind; his hands are raised in his typical story telling gesture, an action my son now endearingly emulates. I'm sure it took more stamina than I imagined, but it was important to him. He strained to chat with co-workers, especially his friend Mark with whom he had worked for many years. Our mutual friends came and celebrated, even with heavy hearts. He opened each card as it was handed to him, and I knew he thought he should not wait to do that.

I had instructed my kids that one of them must always be standing in the entryway to greet guests and say goodbye to them. Our son, Joel, reported afterwards, "Mom, everyone was crying when they left."

My friend Danelle was in tears as she turned to me beside our front door. "I feel like I came to say goodbye to Terry."

I replied, "You did."

I will always be grateful that Terry had those moments at his birthday party to share goodbyes, even if that is not exactly what was talked about.

Our daughter Shauna gave her father a wonderful birthday gift; she provided him with a list of possible names for her baby—Terry chose Audrey Grace as the name for his third granddaughter. Since I was not allowed to see the list, after he selected the name he threw the list in the trash at Starbucks, just another of the stories from Joel's eulogy.

So Terry reached one of his final goals, to turn 55. The other goal was not to be reached, meeting his next two grandchildren.

He died one week and one day after his 55th birthday, three weeks before our granddaughter Audrey made her appearance in our world and four weeks before our grandson Michael.

· 4 ·
WHICH IS HARDER?

As our Younger Bereaved Spouses support group continued to meet month after month, a recurring topic was: "Which is harder: to lose a spouse after a long illness where you had to watch your loved one suffer, or to have a sudden loss where you didn't get to say goodbye?" Of course, we never did come up with a definitive answer for that.

Most of the spouses in the support group had losses that were not sudden. Many of our spouses died of long-term illnesses like cancer. Rhonda and I had both lost our spouses to pancreatic cancer, and for some reason, that gave us a special bond. Only a few had sudden losses such as heart attacks or pneumonia.

Those of us who had spouses with long-term illnesses watched them literally fade away. Terry was always a big man and had spent much of his life on various diets to lose weight, sometimes successful, sometimes not. Before his diagnosis, he weighed close to 240 pounds. The day he died, when Joel helped the hospice worker clean and dress his dad for the last time, Joel said to me later, "Mom, I'm sure he didn't even weigh 120 pounds anymore." It's horrendous watching your spouse decline right before your eyes. Terry's physical decline was dramatic. For this reason, I cannot and will not criticize any man for being overweight. I know that one illness can wipe that out in no time at all. It just isn't important to me anymore.

On the day the oncologist told Terry he was out of options, as we were driving home Terry insisted he must go visit his brother Kim in Houston. This was a week before his birthday and he was already so frail. I was against it at first. The trip to Houston was not long, less than two hours, but the sheer task of getting him to the airport and to his flight was daunting. I relented, and set the wheels in motion for a wheelchair escort and for Kim to be right at the gate when Terry arrived. I could not accompany him because I had already missed a lot of work, and I knew I would be missing more during his last days. It was a tough trip for him; when I picked him up at the airport, an airline employee pushed Terry in a wheelchair where I met them at baggage claim. Terry looked so very weak, as though he could hardly bear the weight of his carry-on bag on his lap. His head was bowed, a gesture that often signaled he was in great discomfort. But it was a last request I am glad I did not deny him.

One of the evenings while Terry was at his brother's, I decided to see a movie by myself. The movie was rather ironically, *The Bucket List*, a story about a terminally ill man who is trying to do everything he always wanted to do before he died. I was wearing my heaviest winter coat as it was a cold day, and I put up the hood and just hunkered down and watched, feeling that I was the only one in the world. I mention that movie because I think it helped prepare me for what was to come. When I think back on sitting alone in that movie theater, I believe I started getting stronger that very night. My own bucket list was about to be drastically revised.

When a person knows death is imminent, that awareness provides some opportunities for the dying person to prepare for the end. They can "put their affairs in order" as the saying goes, make amends, say goodbye. Some who know they are dying choose to create something special to leave behind for the family, such as videos or letters.

If they are so inclined, that is.

Terry was not inclined to talk about his death, or to linger on what we would do without him. I think to him, overthinking it all would be a way of acknowledging that it was going to happen, and he could not do it. When he was first diagnosed, he went to all of his route customers and told them the news. He related his surprise at how many of them were so sad about it. He told them he would be back when he had "beat this thing."

Terry's long-term illness gave people a lot of opportunities to come visit him, and to say goodbye. He was always a storyteller, and he would especially love it when his parents, uncles, brothers, and sisters came to see him. Our living room, where he spent most of his days, resounded with laughter and shared stories. His family was aware that he did not have a lot of time left, and they wanted to make sure he knew he would be remembered.

When they couldn't be there, they would call, and even when his voice got weaker, the family members would fill in the gaps with yet more stories. The hardest phone call was with his mother and sisters about a week before he died. They desired to say an actual goodbye. His mom spoke first. "Terry, it's Mom." His weak reply, "Hi, Mom." I didn't hear any of the rest of the conversation because I could not bear to stay in the room as Joel held the phone to his dad's ear. But I do applaud the family's courage in being able to give him that last call of love.

Years later, when my father lay dying in his memory-care home, I spent the last few days of his life with my sister and nieces. The hospice social worker and I discussed the process of dying and how to say goodbye. She offered her list of "what to say to a dying person." Her list was simple, but after having experienced the loss of Terry, I knew these phrases were comforting for both the dying and those left behind.

What to say to a dying person
> I love you.
> You will be missed.
> I forgive you.
> Please forgive me.
> Thank you.
> It's OK to go.

Though my dad had Alzheimer's and was unresponsive by that time, it gave me solace to use some of these phrases as I sat by his bed. I like to think, on some level, he heard me.

When someone loses a spouse unexpectedly, not being able to say goodbye is very painful.

Mary lost her husband to a heart attack. She shares:

I think back about my sudden loss of Dan and the stories told by my friends in our grief group whose spouses suffered over a length of time. Losing a spouse either way is difficult. I think the difference is that I was not given the chance to say goodbye. I know from hearing the stories of women whose spouses were ill how difficult it was to see them suffer; nevertheless, I was envious of their time to talk, touch, and kiss and say goodbye.

On our ride in the ambulance that night I thought it was going to be a trip to the hospital where the doctor would fix what was wrong. I would get to see Dan when the procedure was over, and he would eventually come home to me. That is what happened before, so why would this time be any different? It proved to be very different.

I walked into the cold operating room after the doctor announced he had tried everything to save my husband's life, but failed. I touched Dan's cold stiff hand and kissed his lifeless lips. And I cried because I didn't get to tell him goodbye.

Also, with an extended illness, the family has time for anticipatory grieving. During Terry's two years of illness, we were aware that he was not going to survive this disease. We had time to prepare somewhat for the eventual day when he would no longer be around.

I was motivated to do some of the pre-planning by the thought of saving my children from the pain of having to deal with those details after their father's death. I was able to do some preparation for the final days and the aftermath, even though Terry was not an enthusiastic participant in this part. He once told me toward the end that it was okay to make funeral and burial preparations, but that he wanted nothing to do with that. Terry had one request: He wanted to be buried in a cemetery plot with a stone. He thought about all the people in his life he had lost and believed there is a certain solace in visiting a gravesite and remembering. I picked an ideal plot. When I reported to Terry the arrangements I had made and asked him if he wanted to visit the spot, he unequivocally declined. Everyone has his own way of coping with loss, and I knew enough to respect his refusal. We never spoke of it again.

He helped me with financial decisions one day just weeks before he died. I had so many questions, and one afternoon I broke down and cried and begged him to go through all of our accounts with me. I think as realistic as Terry was about the seriousness of his illness, he felt that by talking about end-of-life business, his demise would be quickened.

He finally went through everything with me, and called to make sure his life insurance and pension were in order. He sat with me and answered my questions, and gave me advice on what I should do with the life insurance money. At the end of that day, he said to me, "Do you have any more questions?" "No," I replied softly. Then he said in as forceful a voice as his ravaged body allowed him at that point, "Then I don't ever want to talk about this again." He died three weeks later. I do think Terry grieved his imminent death, but in a much different way than I did, of course. He seldom wanted to talk about it, but he did become a bit gentler and less impatient.

I was so appreciative on the day of his death that we had very few arrangements to make. I think perhaps resilience comes a bit sooner for those of us who had time to accept the fact that we were going to be left alone.

I have deep empathy for those who are left suddenly alone without having discussed these issues with their spouses.

Karen shares her story:

My loss was one that came without a bit of warning. Damian and I had been vacationing in Grand Cayman, having the time of our lives, not knowing twenty-nine hours later would be the single worst day of my life. We had gotten home at 3:00 a.m., March 7, 2007. That next evening Damian was already in bed when I brought his cell phone bill to show he had exceeded the "minutes" on his plan. His phone bill was ridiculously high, and since it was our "shared" expense I scolded him, suggesting he watch that more closely. He said he would cover it out of his personal account rather than our joint. I said no, it was okay, but please watch it more closely. I went downstairs to review his bill again only to find 95% of the calls were made to me. I sheepishly and lovingly told him it was okay he went over. It made us both smile, and that would be the last interaction we would ever have.

We turned out the lights just before midnight, and I woke at 7:00 a.m., perplexed to hear Damian's snoring like nothing I had ever heard. He was making noise both inhaling and exhaling. I was surprised at his sounding congested—very congested—yet he hadn't been sick on our trip. I wrestled with whether to wake him and get him to clear his throat, or to let him sleep and call the doctor when he wakes? I scoured the house to find a tape recorder (no smart phones then) to record his breathing. I would bring the recording to the doctor when he wakes. I couldn't get the two I found to work, even replacing the batteries. Forty-five minutes later I poked my head in the bedroom, which was now very quiet. I waited for his snoring; it seemed longer than usual. I softly called his name. No response. I called a little louder. Again no response. I put my hand on his hip and shook him gently. I couldn't breathe, thinking this cannot be happening. Still not fully understanding, I called 911 thinking I didn't care if I was mistaken. I told the operator I thought my husband had died, explaining his breathing and my not being able to wake him. She instructed me to get him on the floor to begin CPR. When I rolled Damian over, his arms flopped like a rag doll. I began CPR, but was having trouble establishing his "airway." Later I would learn he died of pneumonia. His lungs were filled with fluid and there was no possibility of getting air into them.

The EMTs arrived within minutes and took over. Damian was transported to the hospital, but I was not allowed to ride along. Unimaginable. I'm thinking: I can't accompany my husband to the hospital, right now I am incapable of driving myself, AND my husband is dead unless they can revive him. How does this happen when only twenty-nine hours earlier we were sipping fruity drinks in paradise?

In the waiting area the chaplain suggested I shouldn't be alone—wouldn't I like to call someone? I was at a complete loss. Neither of us had family in town, I was only forty-seven years old, and my friends were all at work. I didn't want to bother anyone. This overwhelming aloneness was just a glimpse of what my immediate future was about to be.

The doctor came to explain they had done all they could. Damian had died. They led me into the room and offered me as much time as

I needed. What? Beyond surreal. We had turned out the lights around midnight, basking in the glow from our vacation, and I awoke seven hours later with no husband. I spent two minutes in the hospital room, one and a half minutes longer than I wanted because I felt I should take in the reality of this and say something to him since his spirit would still be present. But he *wasn't there. He was grey, cool to the touch, with an intubation tube sticking out of his mouth. This was not the man I had held in my arms only hours before.*

Completely numb, I was beginning to discover what would be the first of hundreds of decisions to make in roughly forty-eight hours. "Who do you want to handle this?" I was at a complete loss. "Handle what?" "Handle his body." "Um, what?" "Handle his body, you know, prepare the body." "Um, I don't have a clue… do you mean a funeral home?" They respond, "Yes, we have to send his body somewhere." And I reply, "I don't know, can I let you know?" They say I can tell them "now, or in the next hour or so." What? "I was just told five minutes ago my husband is dead, and I have to decide on a funeral home this very moment?" I was still trying to wrap my head around the fact my husband is deceased. They tell me, "That's okay, we need to send him to the coroner first for an autopsy. You can let us know in an hour or so." This cannot be real!

A friend drove me home and I slumped into a chair. How do I even begin the process of calling every single person in each of our lives to notify? I also have about forty-eight hours to singlehandedly plan a funeral and reception worthy of the wonderful man I expected to grow old with.

Damian and I were young. We had never discussed "final wishes." Thankfully he joked about his sensitive skin and needing to be "planted" under a tree. It brought some levity to the most heart-wrenching of tasks. I smile when I see how large that tree has grown and how perfectly it shades Damian's grave—the only wish he lightheartedly asked for. I know he is smiling too.

Widows with sudden losses are forced to deal with unthinkable decisions. How difficult it must be for those who have not had time to discuss the questions that accompany loss: what to do with the body, should there be a burial or cremation, coffin or urn? Where? Should we scatter the ashes in a special place? Now, there is the choice of a "green" or natural burial with minimal environmental impact, one more option added to the seemingly endless list of decisions for a grieving widow.

When a family experiences a sudden loss, these decisions need to be made quickly, adding to the trauma. The pain increases when widows are left dealing with the uncertainty of making a choice they're not sure the deceased loved one would want. If these topics had never been discussed before, it can be daunting. Often, strong emotions of the family can cause additional hurt feelings and harsh words. The abrupt financial mess that accompanies a loss, such as dealing with taxes, house payments, etc., is even more difficult with an unexpected death. It is especially difficult if it was the deceased who always took care of those matters when he/she was alive. A newly bereaving person who is caught off guard can suddenly be faced with not only the shock of the death, but also the realization that she is in charge of it all now. The practical matters require such attention, much less trying to be there for the kids left behind by the loss.

Since our group was for those under the age of 59, many of us had kids who were grown adults, but one man had two kids still in high school. He reported things at group like, "I don't even know how to do laundry;" "Cooking is a mystery to me;" and, "I don't want my kids to see how sad I am, so I cry after they are in bed." The women in our group gave him pointers on laundry and cooking even as we were crying in sympathy for him. Since then he refers to us as "my girls."

So we never did come to a conclusion about "which is harder?" There is not an easy way to let go of someone. The shock of the death is the same. You wake up one morning and realize you are now widowed; and it is permanent, and you must find a way to go on.

· 5 ·
LAST VISITS

IT WAS HARD TO BELIEVE that someone as weak as Terry could live as long as he did. Many times, in that last month, I would ask the hospice nurse, "Do you think this is the end?" She would reply gently, "Yes, but the end can go on for weeks. I don't think he is going to die today."

The hospice had given me instruction booklets on what it would be like in Terry's last days. The booklets talked about how his breathing would change at the end, and ways that we could know the end was near. I made sure all the kids and their spouses read the booklets too. One item mentioned is that, at the end, the dying person will quit breathing frequently, sometimes for up to a minute. When the kids were sitting around the bed, I could often see them look surreptitiously at their watches during these moments. In the last week before he died, the hospice worker suggested they should all gather downstairs and only one or two come up to sit by the bed at a time. She also said they should keep their voices down a bit. "He does not want to leave the party," she explained. It comforted me to hear them down there, as they were all close friends and chatted a lot. One of them would make a coffee run as they passed the time. My daughter-in-law, Ellen, came up once as I was reading some Bible passages to Terry. She sat quietly and listened, her presence comforting.

The hospice had also given me a package to put in the refrigerator, along with instructions, and to not take it out until they told me.

The day after Terry's birthday party, he was weaker than ever, but he still wanted to sit in his favorite chair. About noon, I went to the kitchen to heat some canned beef stew, something he was still able to stomach.

When I returned, he turned stiffly to me, unable to talk. I got him to lie down in the hospice bed, and then called the hospice nurse and Father Marty.

It was time for the package from the refrigerator. The nurse had prepared morphine doses to keep Terry comfortable as he neared the end. Our daughter Shauna volunteered to administer the liquid doses. I agreed to it immediately. (Earlier in Terry's illness, I had given him injections for his low blood count. "I am glad you are a French teacher," he teased, "because you would make a terrible nurse." Eventually, he made the decision to administer the shots to himself. That way, at least he knew what was coming. I was relieved.)

One week after Terry's party, I lay sleeping on the couch next to the hospice bed. Shauna awakened me in the early dawn hours as she gave her father a dose of morphine. After she went back to bed, I returned to the couch and lay awake, listening to the breathing. I lay there, counting the seconds.

"Hey, wait a minute," I remember myself saying.

I leaped up and rushed to Terry. He was not breathing, and did not start. This was the moment he was leaving us.

Later that day, Shauna said to me, "Didn't you feel him above us watching us when we were giving him his last morphine?"

Our daughter Nicole reported that when she got the call, at around 5:20 a.m., four-year-old Emma stumbled sleepily into her room as Nicole was getting ready to leave. Emma said to her mother, "Don't forget to give my sister Alyssa a kiss before you leave."

That was exactly what Terry would say to Emma when we babysat the twins.

"Give your sister Alyssa a kiss."

Both Shauna and Ellen related they each felt great movement of their unborn children at the time of Terry's death that early morning.

I can't help but believe that he visited all four of his grandchildren as he left this world.

Terry and I both loved the singer James Taylor and had seen him in concert. The Saturday before he died, I was alone with Terry and doing some laundry. I put on some of our favorite music, including songs from James Taylor and others. As I was passing by his bed on the way to putting away clothes, the song, "You Can Close Your Eyes," was playing. I paused in my tasks to sit by the bed and softly sang with the music.

So, close your eyes
You can close your eyes, it's all right
I don't know no love songs

And I can't sing the blues anymore
But I can sing this song
And you can sing this song when I'm gone.

Shortly after Terry's death, James Taylor had a concert at Red Rocks, a beautiful concert venue outside of Denver. My friend Cheryl accompanied me to the concert, and it was very emotional to hear the songs that Terry and I had both loved. But he did not sing "You Can Close Your Eyes." The concert ended, and James came out for an encore. Still no "You Can Close your Eyes." I said to myself, "Well, I guess he just is not going to sing that song." Cheryl and I were gathering our things to leave, the crowd was still cheering, and JT came out one more time. He sat on his signature stool casually with his guitar, and no other instruments. Then he began to sing.

Well the sun is slowly sinking down, and the moon is slowly rising. And this old world is still spinning round. And I still love you.

I don't know what inspired James to sing that song at that moment, but I like to think maybe Terry gave him a little nudge.

. 6 .
WHERE DID YOU GO?

With months to prepare and to imagine what it would be like, I still could not believe he was gone.

All of those months, being so strong, and then I did not have the energy to even pick up the phone to call Terry's parents. My young adult children took over, making calls to the rest of the family.

The hospice nurse asked Joel if he would like to help clean his dad's body. As they worked, I stared out the window at the yard Terry always so lovingly tended.

The rest of the family arrived and it was time to call the funeral home. No amount of anticipatory grieving had prepared me for the moment my husband's body would be taken out of our house. I went to our bedroom and lay on the bed. I could not cry.

Joel came in and said, "Mom, are you sure you don't want to be here for this? They are about to take him."

I told him I just could not, and he let me be. I could hear one of my daughter's sobs as they removed Terry's body. When I knew they had left the house, I rejoined my children in the living room.

At the last moment Nicole announced, "I just have to check where they are taking him." She hurried out of the house to watch as they put Terry's body in the vehicle. A few moments later she swept into the house, breathless, and reported, "There were two other bodies in there!" We were used to Nicole's sometimes awkwardly placed observations and this was no exception. Her endearing outburst caused us all to laugh, a light moment we were grateful for.

Later that day, Joel was driving us out to the cemetery to talk about the final resting place, Nicole suddenly piped up from the backseat, "But Mom, what if you decide to remarry? Will you still want to be buried out here?" Joel had heard enough. He said, "Nicole, we are now going to play The Quiet Game" (an activity my mother would do with them when she was taking care of them and couldn't stand the noise anymore). Then he added, "and I want YOU to win."

I don't remember much else about that day except that my kids stayed with me as long as they could. I finally insisted they go home and get some rest.

As they were leaving, Joel turned to me and said, "You're not going to drink now, are you, Mother?"

I thought it was so funny that this is what he was worried about. I told him I would be okay and they left. *And what if I do drink?* I thought. I poured myself a glass of wine and sat in the living room staring at the space where the hospital bed had been.

And that's when the questioning started. The confusion. The pleading.

"You were just here. Where did you go?" "What am I going to

do now?" "Can you just come back for one more day? I forgot to ask you something."

I just could not believe he was gone. It does not matter if it was a long-expected death or a sudden one. The shock of that person being gone is overwhelming.

I was so exhausted I could only drink a sip of the wine and go to bed.

On many days following Terry's death, I could not cry. I was upset about this, and thought there must be something wrong with me. I understood it so much better when I read Elizabeth Berg's line from *The Dream Lover*: "It was much later that I began to see there is a grief for which tears will not come and also a grief for which tears will not stop."

· 7 ·
AM I CRAZY?

AFTER MY LOSS, I was astounded to look around my world and see people simply going about their daily lives as if nothing had happened. I felt I must be the odd one in the world. A world that had little understanding of grief. My sister, Norma, who had lost her first husband at the age of 40, and I marveled at this when we visited the Tattered Cover, her favorite Denver bookstore the day after Terry's funeral. She said, "Just look at all these people who have no idea how your life has changed so radically this week. Life does go on." (She also encouraged me to buy some mandala coloring books for adults. I was very comforted by the activity of coloring and how it allowed me to "just be in the moment" whenever I did it.)

Ultimately, the world is not a safe place to grieve. The world is not comfortable with grieving. In our society, it is common for people to give the bereaved a limited amount of time before they expect it is time to "get over it" and "move on." There is little patience for grief that extends beyond a couple of weeks.

Our support group was a safe place to grieve. We gathered to talk about our lives, forever changed without our spouses. During many sessions, Sarah would have an article copied for us that would get the conversation going. We cried, sometimes sobbed, or wailed.

In this group, no one ever said, "I thought you would be over it by now." "I understand what you are going through; my cat died recently." (Yes, someone did say that to me one day at work!) "How long are you going to stay so sad?" "I thought when I saw you so happy the other day, you were 'over it.'"

One of Mary's neighbors said to her at her mailbox as Mary had a meltdown one afternoon shortly after her husband's death, "I thought you would be on more of an even keel by now." The support group sat in stunned silence when Mary related that story. It was inconceivable to us that anyone could say those words to a new widow. But they do. In the safety of the support group, those kinds of words were never spoken. The group became a place of acceptance, understanding, and empathy.

We all learned the importance of emotional flexibility. All of us had encountered people who simply were not safe for us to be vulnerable with. We found that sometimes, we needed to keep our feelings to ourselves, or to suppress any kind of emotional expression, when we were in the company of those who are not empathetic or supportive. When out in public, and especially when I returned to work, I would plant a smile on my face and make it stay there until I could go home. Many mornings that spring as I finished out the school year, I had to convince myself on the way to work, "You can do this."

After the first few weeks of grief, most of the people in our lives were ready to go back to "normal." People would talk about our "new normal." As Janet said, "I didn't feel normal at all, so I hated that expression."

Our friends and family want us to get to the point where we are the same people we were before this all happened. They want their old friend back.

This is not to be.

The experience of loss changes you forever. The friends who understand this are true and rare indeed. You will get back to "normal," but it won't be the normal everyone was used to seeing in you.

People like it better when you:

Laugh. They feel like that means you are back to normal.

Tell a funny anecdote. They feel like that means you are back to normal.

Decorate for Christmas. They feel like that means you are back to normal. The first year, I did not want to decorate, but I had five grandchildren who would be at Grandma's often over the holidays. My sister Karen said, "Just go buy some new stuff." So, I did.

Go out to a concert, movie, or show. They feel like that means you are back to normal.

Go back to work. They feel like that means you are back to normal.

In our Younger Bereaved Spouses group, we felt anything but normal. In fact, a recurring question posed by one grieving member or another was "Am I going crazy?"

From Janet:
I often remember I thought I was crazy.
Crazy about:
- *the inability to stop crying*
- *the constant desire that it was all a dream and I would wake up and my husband would still be there*
- *not wanting to remove his things from the house*
- *that I hated the saying "it's your new normal," because I didn't feel normal at all*
- *that it hurt more the second year than the first (which I didn't think was possible)*
- *I had to pull over a few times while driving home from our group sessions because I was crying too hard to see where I was driving.*

In one of their monthly newsletters, the Denver Hospice chaplain wrote an article entitled, "You're not crazy." In this article she reminded us that our society has normalized so many crazy behaviors—like lining up at the airport before your flight is called, and gesturing into cellphones—but not grief.

Most people don't know what to do or say following a death. Because of this, many opt to do or say nothing for fear of saying the wrong thing. "There are no words," is a saying people use when they can't find the words to express their sympathy. I understand how difficult it is to come up with the right words, but I appreciated when people tried to empathize, even if it was only with the simple, "I'm sorry." It meant more to me when others attempted to say or do *something*, rather than nothing at all.

During Terry's last weeks, my friend Lana offered to go with me to the cemetery to start the process of picking a plot, and to understand what exactly would happen after the death. I will not forget her kindness.

I was particularly comforted by the floral arrangements people had sent to the funeral home and the church. The funeral director at my church advised me, "Don't tell people not to send flowers. You will be comforted by them." For me, this was true. We had set up a memorial fund where friends and family could donate to pancreatic cancer research and many responded to that. Many sent flowers in addition. I took a great deal of comfort during the visitation at the funeral home and at church reading the accompanying cards and looking at the beautiful arrangements. I still have a peace plant that my cousins sent. I kept all of the sympathy cards, but I don't look at them anymore; they are in a box that will probably be disposed of eventually. But at the time, I read and re-read the sentiments contained in the cards, and truth be told it was difficult for me when cards no longer came in the mail. Some may not care for those outward signs of sympathy, but I gave myself permission to find solace in them.

People assume you are "doing better" if you don't talk about your loss, but I found that it is okay to let them know you want to talk about it, and it will not upset you if your spouse's name is mentioned. For most of my friends, it was a relief to be able to talk about Terry, as they missed him too and wanted to reminisce.

It is still hard to look back at that time. I can still conjure up the same feelings that I had more than ten years ago when I think of the weeks and months surrounding the loss.

Rhonda on grieving:

I feel it is important in grieving to allow yourself to grieve…cry, lie in bed, eat bad food, talk to nobody. The days that you feel this way will lessen. Even after time has passed and one of these days comes upon you, just let it pass through you as you feel the sorrow. Everyone is different in how they grieve and you have to be respectful of that.

Mary shares:

So I was known as the late night shopping diva amongst the Sistahs. I could not sleep very well and instead of counting sheep, I began tuning into the infomercials. It was addicting. One of my first purchases was a Core Rhythms Dance Exercise Program, and since I loved watching Dancing with the Stars, *I felt like it would be a great investment. I could stand to lose some weight and looking at the before and after pictures encouraged my purchase even more. Needless to say, the videos are still in their original wrappers and I eventually found other ways to channel those sleepless nights.*

. 8 .
MAGICAL THINKING

IN JOAN DIDION'S BOOK, *The Year of Magical Thinking,* she writes about the difficulty in believing that your loved one is really gone. It helped me to know that others had the same sensation that our loved ones might just come back.

Subconsciously, I thought if I were "good" enough, or "strong" enough, Terry would maybe come back. Totally irrational, I know, but at the time it was so real.

One day shortly after the funeral, Nicole noticed a pair of Terry's shoes sitting by the patio door.

"Don't you think you should put those shoes away?"

Without thinking, I said, "Well, I don't know, he may need them sometime."

Nicole gave me a strange look, but said nothing.

Magical thinking. Many of us had that experience during the early months of that first year.

I occasionally felt Terry's presence, heavily, during certain events.

In December of the year Terry died, our twin granddaughters,

Alyssa and Emma, were in a kindergarten Christmas program. I was not able to attend the program, so my daughter arranged for me to see it at the school performance earlier in the day with the grade school and the teachers. I walked into the auditorium before the program. The schoolchildren were all seated on the floor. I sat at the end of the empty row of chairs behind them. The program started and the kindergartners started to sing, "Christmas is in Your Heart," complete with the gestures so dear to kindergarten performers.

Suddenly I felt an intense presence next to me. It was as if Terry had walked in and sat beside me for that song. I leaned slightly to the chair on my left and whispered, "You're here, aren't you?" The song ended and the feeling of the presence dissipated.

That same year, my kids made plans to meet me at our church for Christmas Eve Mass. I arrived earlier than the rest of the family, and went in to sit down and save places for them. Nicole arrived at some point after me. She spoke briefly with Father Marty, asking him if he had seen her mom.

He said, "Yes, she is wearing a red sweater." Nicole laughed at this and mentioned how most women her mom's age wore red sweaters at Christmastime. Just at that moment, she said to Father Marty, "Oh, never mind. I see my dad, so there she is."

I don't know what Father Marty's reaction was, but Nicole felt she absolutely saw Terry for a moment sitting beside me.

Janet wrote:
I had several experiences that made me feel Dave was still here. Once in a dream an angel swooped by and wrapped me up in a golden

blanket…very warm. Considering it was January, or February, it was extremely comforting. Another time I awakened to an "angel" kissing me. The most explicit visit was a night I was babysitting our only granddaughters at the time, and in the middle of the night I went into their room to check on them. When I turned around Dave was standing in the doorway. I gave him a hug and he hugged me. I could even smell him. I don't remember him saying anything, or what I said. But that was one of the last encounters I remember. Made me feel very good.

People sometimes related to me that they had had a dream about Terry after he died. For some reason, this always made me feel sad, as I had had no dreams of him. I read somewhere that perhaps the person who died is not coming to you in a dream because he is leaving you alone to deal with the reality of his passing.

My friend Anne, a former neighbor, had very generously delivered several meals to us when Terry was ill, including desserts, which she knew he loved. Terry died during my spring break from teaching, and Anne, also a teacher, was on a cruise during that week. One night, she woke from a dream about Terry where he said at the end of the dream, "Well, Anne, I have to go now. Happy Saint Patrick's Day." Anne startled awake. Happy Saint Patrick's Day? That was a few days ago. She told her husband that she needed to go to the computer room on the ship and look at the newspaper. Sure enough, she found out that Terry had died on St. Patrick's Day.

Rhonda wrote:

About six months after Mike passed I was blow-drying my hair. I glanced over towards the doorway of the bathroom and there stood

Mike, so clear. I was breathless for a moment and crumbled. And then he was gone. I sobbed for some time.

The magical thinking gradually faded away, and we were left to figure out how to live our lives without our beloved. The new reality was that those shoes would not be worn again; we would never attend the grandkids' sports games, recitals, and school programs together; and our husbands would never again stand in the doorway, watching us get ready. It seemed an insurmountable reality to face.

· 9 ·
MISSING THE DECEASED

THE HOSPICE ARRANGED skilled therapists to work with our support group. Our first social worker, Sarah, was young and although she didn't have personal experience with grief, she exuded empathy, her face always reflecting our pain as we shared our feelings and experiences week after week.

One topic that came up often was how much we missed the sound of our spouse's voice around the house. We had different ways of coping with that.

My son Joel sounds so much like his dad, and has gestures so much like Terry's that I felt a piece of him was still with me. Rhonda's husband had made an audio production with the aid of a friend when they knew he was dying. She has this precious memento of Mike talking and reminiscing on tape.

Wrote Rhonda,

Mike was a very smart man and he did a lot of philosophizing, but also told lots of stories about his early life and gave advice to the kids.

It is special to just hear his voice. He had a great voice.

Many of us in our group were envious of Rhonda's tapes. A few had home movies they still could not bear to watch. Others talked about recorded phone messages, how they could not remove them from their phones; many told how they listened to those messages almost every day. Some held on to the recorded greeting with their spouse's voice still on it. Of course, this tends to creep people out when they call you and hear your deceased spouse's voice on the message. Nothing we can do about that, we decided in the group.

One session, after we had talked about this topic for a while, Sarah mentioned she had a video clip from the movie, *P.S. I Love You,* that she would bring in the next time.

It was the only thing that Sarah did for our group that turned out to be a disaster.

The following week, Sarah played the clip of the young wife played by Hilary Swank, who had tragically lost her husband. Often Swank's character would crawl under the covers of her bed with her cellphone just to listen over and over to his recorded voice. Watching this clip, our group crumbled one by one. By the time the clip was over, we were all sobbing and could hardly look up.

Sarah looked at us with her incredibly empathetic countenance and muttered. "Well, maybe that wasn't such a good idea after all."

It was just the thing to bring us back to the moment. We laughed and wiped our tears and laughed again.

One can find healing in a most unexpected form. When Terry died, our daughter Nicole was looking for books that would explain his death to her four-year-old twin daughters. She arrived at my house one day with the book, *Tear Soup*, which was originally written for children, saying she thought I would find it helpful as well. It is beautifully illustrated and simple in its ability to comfort and console. Of all the books I read, and I did a lot of reading, *Tear Soup* was a book I turned to for comfort time and again. I was delighted during support group when Deb mentioned this little treasure.

I was once requested by the group to bring my copy of *Tear Soup* to our next session, and I read it to them. Tears rolled down the cheeks of the group members as they listened. I have since given this book to several newly bereaved friends. Since it is not long, and is illustrated so beautifully, it is perfect for grieving people who do not have a long attention span and cannot focus for a very long period of time.

This lovely book gives you permission to grieve, and then heal.

Once, Karen came to a group session when she had not been there for a few months. The first anniversary of her husband's death was approaching.

Karen shares her memories of that meeting:

I cried and cried, and could barely get the words out that I felt I was seeing my life with Damian through the rear-view mirror, and I so didn't want that. I wanted to hang onto my life with him, and I saw it slipping further and further behind me. I had this with my mother's death too. The end of the first year was a very difficult time period. I was no longer numb and people no longer asked much about my loss, or how I was doing. Their lives had moved on, and I was in the depth of my deepest grief—not "raw," just deep.

This was a group of acceptance and understanding. She knew we would not say, "Get over it, it's been a year." It was a place of consolation and comfort. We all knew the deep grief of missing our beloved.

. 10 .
PLACE TO REMEMBER

For most bereaved, there is a place to go where they can evoke memories of their loved ones after the final goodbye. For many cremation took place and the ashes were scattered or placed in an urn in a formal memorial wall. For some the ashes were scattered in a place that was special to the loved one. Mary had a bench placed at the Mother Cabrini shrine outside of Denver, which she visited frequently. For me the cemetery is a place I can go to be comforted and to remember.

Terry and I always liked Starbucks. The coffee shop in our neighborhood took on a special meaning in his life as his disease progressed. He was no longer able to continue working, even though in the first year he had hopes of returning to work, even buying himself a new lunch box with special thermoses and containers to hold the foods that he could still stomach. He didn't lose his taste for coffee until the very end. When he got to the point in his illness where he could no longer work and should no longer be driving, he would still get in his vehicle when I was at work and drive the one and a half blocks to the neighborhood Starbucks. The employees there got to know him well, and treated him kindly. They would have his drink ready for him when he slowly made his way into the coffee shop: a "venti vanilla latte with five raw sugars."

After he died, when I would visit his grave, I would occasionally take that beverage to his stone and leave it there. The first time I ordered his favorite coffee after Terry died, my barista gave me a sad sympathetic look and asked if I was all right. He knew that was Terry's drink and not mine. I took it out to the cemetery and placed it on the grave, something that I did with some regularity in those first months. My sister Karen used to joke that the cemetery workers probably hurried over to Terry's grave when they saw me leave so they could enjoy a nice coffee.

The Starbucks staff loved Terry so much, that later on the morning that he died, I went over to get coffee for myself and told the manager, Ron, that Terry had died. I have never seen a retail staff be so kind and caring. Seven of them even came to his funeral. A testament to Terry's horrible weight loss over the two years: when they were looking at the photo boards that my kids had prepared for the funeral, Ron said to his staff, "Hey, this guy comes to Starbucks too." His staff had to tell him that the man on the board was Terry, the same man who spent his last year using Starbucks as his last link with the outside world.

At first I would go to the cemetery often, several times a week. Terry's gravesite is a beautiful spot. The mountains in the distance are sometimes purple, sometimes white, but the site itself is on the prairie. When the wind blows you can hear the grasses move, reminding me of our roots in North Dakota. Here, I could be alone with my thoughts and memories. And my tears and sometimes even my wailing. I would arrive at Terry's stone, place some flowers, and trace his name on the stone, remembering the good and bad times. I had a playlist of our favorite songs on my phone, and I would sit on the lawn and lean back on the stone. Sometimes tears would pour down my face, and other times it got more vocal. I would sob at the unfairness of it all.

On the first Memorial Day after Terry died, my mother-in-law Helen, who still lived in North Dakota, asked me if I would please go to a store and purchase some plastic flowers for Terry's grave, a common tradition for people of her generation. She asked me to take a picture of the grave with the flowers. I said I would, but silently I fretted at the idea. I would never put plastic flowers on a grave if I had my choice. My sister Bev was visiting that weekend and I told her what Helen had asked. She said, "Well, let's just go and see what is out there." We went to Michael's, the craft store, and I wandered around in tears as I thought to myself: *I am too young to be picking out plastic flowers for my husband's grave.* I just could not do it. We went to get fresh flowers and drove back to the grave.

I was wracked with guilt for not fulfilling Helen's wishes as I placed the fresh flowers in the vase at the grave. Bev, who could see I was melting down, spotted a plastic arrangement on a nearby grave, picked it up and placed it on Terry's grave, snapped a picture, and returned the bouquet to where it belonged. It was just the funny moment I needed to stop feeling sorry for myself.

I later went back to Michael's and found a beautiful silk arrangement that I could live with and that I knew Helen would like. I took a picture, mailed it to her and never told this story to anyone (until now). Now when I visit the grave, I remember the raw emotion of those first years. I am now able to visit the grave without crying and sobbing; it is a calming, serene spot where I can go to remember. I am so grateful.

· II ·
GUILTY RELIEF

You start to mark the chronology of your life as "before" and "after" the death of your spouse.

Caretaking had been exhausting. The worry was overwhelming. Driving home from school on Friday afternoons during the two years of Terry's illness, I would be in tears thinking of the weekend ahead and the fatigue I would feel being with him constantly while still trying to get papers graded, laundry done, and medications administered. When it was all over, after Terry died following two and a half years of illness, there was a relief and calm.

And guilt.

Yes, I felt relief that my spouse's suffering was over, but I felt guilty about the relief I felt, that my exhaustion from caregiving would finally be relieved. I felt guilty when I finally got a good night's sleep. I would even feel guilty if I allowed myself to laugh. What was I doing enjoying my life when my poor husband was no longer here to enjoy it with me?

You have to learn to forgive yourself for going on living. That was hard for me at first when I would remember how Terry railed against "the dying of the light," and wanted to live so badly.

Then it starts to seem so long ago that sometimes you cannot remember very clearly what it was like before he died. And that can be a scary thing. I panicked when sometimes for a second I could not conjure up his face in my mind, or remember the sound of his voice. My friend Marge says, "I don't think about him much anymore and that sometimes makes me feel sad and guilty." But it is a healthy thing not to have those thoughts at the back of your mind on a daily basis. It shows that you are functioning in your life. Most of us know deep down that our spouses would be glad for that.

I didn't lose the love when I lost Terry. I just had to come up with new ways to become the new person I was becoming. I had to learn to be gentle with myself. I had to relearn how to plan and dream.

I read everything I could about grief and grieving. I needed to become knowledgeable about this new phase of my life. I listened to other people. Many times, I took their advice with a grain of salt, but at least they were talking to me.

Grief is not a constant state. I had to give myself permission to live life again, to find happiness. I had to acknowledge my feelings of grief before I could move on to find relief.

You change so much after the loss of a spouse. No longer are you married, even though you had been for maybe decades. You are no longer part of "we." You no longer wake up on your birthday, or Valentine's Day, or your anniversary, anticipating how you will spend the day with your loved one.

And then one day, it hits you. You realize your spouse is not coming back. You make small decisions here and there to "get back out there" into the world that has changed so much for you. You decide you have to make your own happiness, it is not going to come looking for you. Being with the support group gave me new ways to find happiness again. It became apparent that happiness was not going to find me without some effort on my part. You still hurt, a lot, and memories that flood back threaten to return you to that place where you can't move.

But gradually those memories start making you smile, or you allow yourself to acknowledge memories where maybe it wasn't all great all of the time. It does not make you feel guilty; it is just acknowledging the reality of your once-married life.

. 12 .
NEW LIFE STRATEGIES

Around that table at the hospice, I could feel people testing the waters of what it would be like to go on loving and living. At our monthly dinners, we observed our progress of adjusting to our new environments. Some moved to new homes, picked up new hobbies, and in general, we all were trying to learn how to live life in this new world of ours.

Each facet of grief had to be attended to: the physical acceptance of the loss, as well as all of our emotional, spiritual, and psychological reactions. It helped to exercise regularly and eat well. At first, my body felt as if I could not move if I tried. And then, later, I could start to walk again and get to the gym. Several of the group went on hikes together, giving us the opportunity not only to exercise, but to talk through our life situations with each other.

Eating regularly was a problem. I had to accept again the reality that there was no longer anyone coming home at the end of the day to share a meal with me. Sometimes, I would forget to eat, which still amazes me. The rotisserie chickens at Costco were a lifesaver. I would buy one and use it for the week in salads and other dishes. I could eventually start working toward a normal pattern of eating. It was important to finally feel that I had my physical strength back.

    To experience grief is actually to go on a personal spiritual journey. In this period of my life, I reexamined my philosophy of life, my goals, my values, and beliefs. Terry's death led me to question my spiritual beliefs. I just had such a hard time accepting he was gone, and I didn't know to where. My faith tradition told me that he was in heaven, and I had never thought so much about that until after he died. I continued to attend church, but it took me a long time for my faith to return, and when it did, it was different. Talking to other widows over the years, I found this to be a normal reaction, and though many of us continued to go to church, we were just not sure anymore. The death of a loved one forces you to confront those existential questions that you may have avoided before: What really happens when you die? Why am I here and he is not? You find yourself confronting questions that you used to avoid, going through your busy daily life. Bereavement can shift your daily perspective and force you to think about life in whole new ways. I read somewhere that we should be thankful for all of our emotions, even the sad ones, and that helped me somewhat. Some people never do go back to their previous faith traditions, but discover other ways to find spiritual solace.

    Sometimes it was all I could take to handle my own emotions. I just could not be there for everyone. I learned to ask for help, realizing that many of my friends just wanted to do something to help and this was a concrete request I could give them. It helped to be kind to myself and to do only what I could handle.

One of the things Terry had suggested to me was to put in a sprinkler system and a garage door opener, which we had been able to live without up until now. I don't remember how I got the sprinkler system installed, but somehow I made all the calls and it got done. The garage door was a different story. A dishonest handyman tried to talk me into doing more jobs for me, and it wasn't until my son intervened that I saw what was going on. I had so wanted to show my family that I was okay. From then on, I relied on friends to help me find reliable and reputable people to help me around the house. My friends Karen and Bobbie offered to paint my bedroom a buttery yellow and helped me with new bedding. My friends Susan and Jerry were there for me so often and completed a bathroom remodel, helping me every step of the way. Terry and I had never had much money for remodeling, so I was rather clueless about picking colors, tile and the like. My new life became a little easier to manage when I admitted it was okay to ask for help.

· 13 ·
VALUE OF GROUP

IF I COULD GIVE ONE PIECE of advice to a newly bereaved friend, I would tell her to find a group of like-minded and safe people to be with. People who have experienced a similar loss are the safest people to be with.

They "get you" when you burst into tears talking about the special holiday activities you enjoyed as a couple. They "get you" when you say that you crawled into bed with your husband's cardigan sweater, hoping for just a little bit of the scent to come through. They "get you" when you say that you stayed up all night and maybe ordered a thing or two that you didn't need on an all-night shopping channel just to hear a nonjudgmental voice on the phone. They "get you" when you tell them that you simply cannot throw away the last Valentine's card you ever received from your spouse even though it's been two years, and you still put an old birthday card on your pillow on your birthday to pretend he is still there. In our support group, no one cares how many times you bring up the same story as you try to accept the reality of your new life.

During one particularly emotional session at our Younger Bereaved Spouses support group, I moaned, "I don't know why I keep coming to this when I am just so emotionally wrung out by the end of the session."

Rhonda replied, "Well, when you are at home, do you look forward to coming back?" We all knew the answer to that. We couldn't wait to come back.

During the meetings, we generally would be given some kind of reading that would encourage discussion, reflection, and memories. The meeting closed when our two hours were up, and Sarah was great at leading us to closure. She would announce when the next session would be held, in two weeks on a Wednesday. If there happened to be five Wednesdays in the month, we would be reminded that it would be three weeks before we met again. There was an audible groan every time Sarah mentioned this, as we all counted the days until our next session.

We talked openly about a myriad of issues that faced us as we set out into the world in a way we didn't dream we would have to just a few years earlier. For instance, I never imagined what it would be like to get out the Christmas decorations and put up the tree by myself. The first year I just could not do it. I bought new stuff as my sister Karen suggested instead of delving into the memory pit of the basement storeroom that year. It was just so much better to do that. The holidays are fraught with emotional memories, and I did not need to go there on purpose. Just hearing a Christmas song on the radio that reminded me of Terry could set me back several hours. When I shared this in the group, heads were nodding, and I knew I was not alone.

Before Terry got sick, I never imagined the stress that could be caused by having to deal with all the financial tasks ahead of me. I was lucky to have over two years of anticipatory grieving and to finally be able to sit down with Terry to talk about it, as reluctant as he was. When the support group talked about these types of financial challenges, I learned to truly listen to and feel what other people were saying. I had so much empathy for those who didn't have that preparation time.

We all looked forward to these biweekly sessions. As Bob stated, "There were weeks when I counted the minutes until I could be together with this group." It didn't take us long to realize that the only way we could still put one foot in front of the other was to keep coming to this group.

Rhonda says:

I went to my first support meeting in February 2007. Mike had passed in January 2007. I did nothing but cry the whole time. When my time came to share my loss, I could not because all I could do was cry. I left feeling horrible. I attempted again in June 2007 and the meeting became my lifeline. My whole life was scheduled around attending these meetings…, I so looked forward to seeing everyone. I still cried a lot, especially in the beginning, but was able to finally talk. This was a place where I could be totally understood because everyone was feeling similar things. I could talk about anything…when to take off my wedding ring, when to go through Mike's stuff. I do remember feeling appalled that some of the men whose loss was fairly recently were talking about wanting to date. I was not anywhere close to that. This was a safe place to talk and cry.

Mary wrote:

I had gone back to work two weeks after Dan had passed. I am pretty sure that I did not look like the former me as my eyes were red and puffy and little things would set me off. My colleagues gave me a wide berth and tried to be sympathetic and kind. One of my colleagues was married to a counselor at Denver Hospice. He was very concerned as Dan had passed away so suddenly that I had no outside support. He was pretty persistent in sharing his thoughts about my joining a grief group and of course since his wife worked at Denver Hospice, he had access to their schedule of sessions. Each day he would "kindly" point to one of the sessions and say, I really think this might be good for you. After another month or so I began to listen to him seriously. There was one session that met on Wednesdays twice a month that was a drop-in session for younger bereaved spouses. It looked like it might be one I could relate to. I attended one snowy evening in March, much to my family's worrisome reactions, and was so thankful for my colleague's persistence. Not sure where I would be today without the love and support of the group that I met that night and continue to keep in close contact with.

Debbie shares:

Because I had felt the comfort of being in a support group, I looked into the support group for newly bereaved younger spouses. Rhonda had mentioned that she had gone to one session, but never went back.

I gave it a try in July and she agreed to go with me after that. There is something to be said for being in a room when someone says something about their experience and the entire room nods their heads. I knew no one else who had gone through my experience and there was a force drawing me back meeting after meeting. Once I went the first time, it became a regular part of my schedule. Even when my grief had settled, I felt I could help others just beginning their journey, just as others had helped me.

· 14 ·
JOLLY GROUP

AFTER TWO HOURS of pouring out our hearts, when the session was over, several members of our Younger Bereaved Spouses support group would gather at a nearby restaurant for appetizers, or dinner. At first when I was invited I couldn't bear to go. How could they throw off that mantle of grief so quickly and go out to eat and drink?

I had been with the group for about four weeks, when I finally thought, *Why not? What else have I got to go home for?* I was grateful that Lynne, who invited everyone every time, did not give up on me.

And I understood after the first dinner that this ritual also served an important purpose: It was a place where we reentered the world after the emotional support group time.

Not everyone would go every week, but there were usually at least ten to fifteen of us at dinner. One week only one of the men attended the after-dinner. When we arrived at the restaurant, the hostess asked how many there were of us. She then looked at us and said to Wayne, "Wow, you are really lucky tonight with all these women." Wayne replied, "Yeah, and they're all single!"

One time we were heading to our table, about twelve of us, and Rhonda was stopped by a friend whom she had not seen in a long time. The friend had not heard of Rhonda's husband's death. "Who is that jolly group you are with tonight?" That name stuck. It was a testament to our ability to leave the group setting fractured and weeping, and to go out and face the world laughing and joking. We called ourselves the Jolly Group for a long time afterward. We often talked about how we sure fooled people. If they had only seen us an hour earlier.

I was sitting next to a woman one week at dinner, and she took a call from her daughter (we often were interrupted by our kids as they were dealing with their own grief issues.) She listened to her daughter on the phone, nodding and murmuring. Finally, I heard her say, "You need a grief group!"

It was so early in our time together, and while others could not see how we could be out laughing and talking after our group sessions, we understood how important it was for our reentry into the world.

· 15 ·
THE POWER OF LISTENING

Our support group became a place where we could talk and no one tried to one-up each other. I found I could learn so much just by listening to what others had already experienced, and never once do I remember wishing that someone would hurry up and finish so I could jump in. I always knew my turn would come.

In other places in our lives, people who had not been through the same experience wanted often to "help" instead of listen. That is a human reaction. Well-intentioned friends or family members try to relate to what we have been through, to bring us comfort. When someone would say, "I understand exactly how you feel," but she still had her husband, her words only brought me more suffering rather than the comfort I know she intended.

People have all sorts of advice for you when you have had a profound loss. "Don't make any major decisions in the first year," is one of the most popular. You receive so much unsolicited advice when you are in this raw stage of life, and often at support group we would roll our eyes at the absurd counsel well-meaning people offer to widows:

"What are you going to do about your house, finances, life? Are you sure you want to do that so soon?"

"Everything happens for a reason." This is my personal most-hated expression. It seems very spiritual to say this, but for the grieving person who already has to handle the shock of the loss, it may give them more anxiety as they try to figure out what the "reason" is.

"God never gives you more than you can handle." Once again words meant to give solace, but it made me wonder what I had done for God to think I was strong enough to handle this.

Looking back, I think people sometimes say these platitudes in hope that it won't happen to them. "I could never be as strong as you (so maybe God won't ever give me this cross to bear)."

To a freshly grieving widow like I was at the time, anything short of listening fell short. The last thing I needed to hear was unsolicited advice or false words of empathy. I appreciated simple words of sympathy—"I'm so sorry…," "I'm here if you need me,"—but I could do without the advice. Yet, I was grateful that I had friends who cared. Advice is given because it is frustrating for people to think there is nothing they can do to help.

I like what John Pavlovitz says about the topic:

"Relatively soon you will likely encounter a grieving person you love, whose devastation shakes you and whose heart you will want to heal with words.

"This is a beautiful aspiration, just know that it is a likely an impossible one.

"Be quick to embrace.
"Be urgent in presence.
"Be very slow to speak."

In our support group we were reminded to listen without judgment and not try to compare, give advice, or "help" in any way, but to listen. In our two-hour sessions, we would take several breaks, especially if it was a particularly heart-wrenching session. During those breaks, when I first joined, many would come up to me and say simply that they could feel my pain. Wayne said, "I just hurt so bad for you just listening. I am sorry." And these were people who were going through a similar life experience. I learned a lot about empathy during those sessions. They weren't trying to compare my situation to anything they had suffered, like the woman at school who tried to empathize by telling me her cat died so she knew how I felt. Nobody in the group, ever, said, "Well listen to my story, and it's worse than yours." All I could see around that table were eyes full of empathy and understanding. It went a long way to help my healing.

With time, we all began to recognize comforting phrases and questions that felt like gold, infinitely more helpful than uninvited advice.

- "How are you doing *today*?" This is such a kind thing to ask. It is agonizing to always have to come up with an answer to, "How are you?" You feel like you have to say, "Fine," or "Okay," when you are really not. This adding of "today" gives grieving people more opportunity to share what they are going through and lets them know you are sincerely interested in what today is like for them. "Well, not so great. I broke down at the store when I saw Terry's favorite cereal." Or, "Well, I had to go to the Social Security office today. That was no fun." (I was bewildered when the Social Security Administration issued me a check for $250 as a death benefit. When I told my mom over the phone about this, she said, "Oh yes, they used to call that the burial benefit." I replied, "You can't even bury a groundhog for that." We laughed over the absurdity of it all.)

- "Tell me about your spouse. What was he/she like and how did you know he/she was 'the one'?"
- "I am so sorry for your loss. I can't imagine how you feel."
- "There is no timeline for your grief, and I will listen to you whenever you need to talk."
- "Do you need help with anything around the house? Let's make a list of unfinished tasks that you want to get done." My friends Lisa and Michael, and John and Kath, came over one Saturday, tools and lumber in tow, and built shelves and cabinets in my garage—something I desperately needed to help get my life organized, which usually calms me and makes me feel like I am coping. It was Michael's idea, no surprise, as men often need to do something practical instead of just talking.
- "We are going to a (restaurant, movie, concert, church, etc.). Would you like to join us? We will come and get you and bring you home when you are ready."

Losing a spouse at any age is not a unique experience, but when it happens to you, you often feel you are alone in your grief. With the support of the other widows and widowers in my group, I was able to make my way through that lonely place to the "other side of sadness." When I hear that someone I know has just experienced this loss, I can literally feel his or her pain. I hope by listening and offering sincere words of comfort I can help them, in at least some small way, just as my support group has helped me.

. 16 .
911/411

The first 911 From Mary:

I decided to go out to the cemetery as I was melancholy and missed Dan. I drove to Mt. Olivet, walked over to the stone, and looked up at the sky with the geese flying overhead. I looked down and saw his name chiseled into the cold granite. I looked all around at all of the stones with dates of young people and old people.

I knelt down and sprayed holy water on the ground and prayed, an old tradition that I witnessed my mother doing all of the times we went to the cemetery near where I grew up. I kept thinking how it was my turn to spray the holy water.

I left the cemetery and drove home and sat in my car and struggled with the emotions I was feeling. I sent out a text to the "Sistahs" that I was in need of some love and talk time and titled it "911."

I got immediate responses from Sunny, Deb, Janet, Jan, and Sue. It was that fast and we were to meet at Champs. I was surrounded by my new best friends and their love and I felt I could breathe again.

This was the first 911 with more to follow.

We used the 911 call to reach each other when we were feeling like we couldn't handle what was going on that day. If we were having a particularly bad day, we could send an email to the group with the subject line "911." Within minutes, the group would respond, and more often than not, quickly decide on a gathering place for a happy hour where we could hash over the latest happenings. The 911 was used for such minor events as someone saying something thoughtless that would send us into sobs, or a big thing like an anniversary that we just couldn't cope with that day.

Sometimes it was as simple as being asked out on a date and not knowing how to respond. Other times, it was a realization that your in-laws were not communicating much with you anymore. We were able to conclude with that one that just our being alive reminded them of their dead loved one, and it was hard to have the same relationship. That got better over time, and the phone calls with my mother-in-law became an event I looked forward to as she passed on family news that I might not have heard about otherwise.

Sometimes it was just driving by an old familiar place that would throw us into a tailspin. Many in the group stayed in the same house they shared with their spouse for years. Therefore being in the same neighborhood where we lived our married lives brought new occasions for grief. I still can't drive by the Dairy Queen on Colfax in Denver without remembering the Tuesdays that Nicole would bring Terry a DQ milkshake because "the shakes were the best there." I can hardly drive by the KFC in my old neighborhood without thinking of one of the last foods he could eat. For some reason, greasy fried chicken seemed to settle his pain.

From Deb:

Yup, familiar places. I remember the time I was walking by Brant's "favorite" store at Cherry Creek Mall. They had some scented candles wafting into the mall (I know Brant hated candles, it was the scent that got me). The fragrance had me sobbing in the middle of the mall. Oh, those damn bursts of grief will get you, no warning, no matter where you are.

Nothing was too big or small for a 911 call; it was just that something had happened that you needed a little extra support for. And, of course it was another excuse for a happy hour.

Eventually, we also developed the 411 call. If someone had some special news to share, it was a 411 call that brought us together. It could be a big event like someone finally admitting they were dating, (me!) to a life event such as an adult child's job success, a new grandchild, or a decision to try online dating. The 411 is where we would announce things to the group that seemed life-changing, and we just had to share with these special people. It became a less-urgent type of call, just wanting to share news with friends who understood. I think all in all, our 411s were just another excuse to gather and laugh and cry together, and to reassure ourselves that we really were not "crazy" and, even more importantly, that we were not alone.

. 17 .
LETTING GO

OVER TIME THERE WERE periods that, when I look back on them, were significant in my decision to move forward.

One of them was the removal of Terry's personal effects from our closet and our home. To someone who has not been through this, it might seem crass that I would ever want to remove the clothing, the mementos, the reminders of the person with whom I had shared 33 years of my life. But to someone who has been through this, you understand that to keep all of these things around eventually makes you feel "stuck;" you can't function daily if every time you walk into your shared closet, you are faced with the clothing, the smells, and the overwhelming memories.

The timing is individual for each person. For me the removal of Terry's clothes from our closet came fairly soon after he died. In the two and a half years preceding his death, I had imagined many times what it might be like to have to take down his clothes and give them away. My sister Bev was in town shortly after the funeral, and one day she asked, "Would you like me to help you go through Terry's things?"

At first I was shocked anyone would think I would want to do that so soon. But I knew that it was the right time for me. We opened the closet and started with a couple of bags that I would take to Goodwill, or another donation place. It was heartrending. Bev told me that I should save some pieces that meant something special to me, and also we decided to save about a dozen shirts.

Years ago, when my brother-in-law Arnie died a sudden death, one of his daughters took many of his shirts and found someone who would make teddy bears out of the shirts as keepsakes for many of us. I wanted to do that with some of Terry's shirts, too. My daughter Nicole later found a website where she could send the shirts and she had bears made for me and for her siblings. I was at work the day she sent me pictures of the bears that had been made. I opened her email not expecting what I was about to see. There, lined up in a row, sat six bears fabricated from the shirts we so often saw Terry wearing. Another unexpected wave of grief poured over me. And then, I had to shut down my email and go teach a class!

As I took each shirt from its hanger, I held the fabric to my nose and inhaled deeply. I knew the scent of Terry would not remain for long on the clothing, and I didn't want to let it go. He was a smoker, which I always hated, but the scent of him was so strong on the clothes that I couldn't believe he wasn't still with us. I decided to keep some pieces besides the shirts. I told myself it was for the kids if they should ever want them.

Those pieces hang in my closet still today: the cream-colored cardigan sweater that he wore around the house all the time, and even more so in the last year when he was always cold. I even remember when he bought that sweater on a trip to Minneapolis at least twenty years before. In the first year after his death, I wore that sweater to bed and around the house for comfort.

Another piece I saved that still hangs in my closet is Terry's Civil War sweatshirt. I gave it to him for Christmas one year. He was a big Civil War history buff, and he loved that extra large sweatshirt. I have never worn it, but I will save it for a grandson who might enjoy having it someday. Another saved item, a three-piece blue suit that Terry bought for a special occasion early in our marriage. We never had a lot of money, and this was a huge purchase for us. He couldn't wear it in the past twenty years, as his weight had changed, but always saved it as a memory. Joel took the suit, and the jacket fits him perfectly. He recently wore it to a cousin's wedding, a nice retro piece.

I saved every one of Terry's white undershirts, and still wear one to bed occasionally and have used them as painting smocks for the grandkids. I always tell them whose shirts those were; there are so many ways to keep your loved ones' memories alive.

I don't remember how long the scent of Terry lingered on the clothes. But I do remember that I would bury my nose in my bear, and still faintly smell the scent of cigarettes. (These were all laundered clothes, but the scent of smoke does not go away easily.)

After Bev and I finished the clothing task, I started, over a period of days, to go through Terry's personal items: his wallet, his dresser drawer of items. He was not a materialistic person, and unlike his wife, did not save a lot of things. I placed these items in brown a grocery bag and labeled it, For the Kids to Go Through and Throw Away the Rest. I planned to give them their bag the following week.

It didn't happen: My cleaning lady saw the bag and evidently thought it was her task to dispose of the bag when she was cleaning the next day. I was horrified to come home one day, look for the bag and discovered it was gone. I immediately called the cleaning lady, and she remembered throwing it away. My emotions were unleashed, and I could not believe she had done this. When I look back on it now, I know it was my fresh grief that contributed to my anger that day.

The trash had been collected already by the time I discovered that bag missing and calls to the waste disposal company yielded not much hope. It was Nicole who assured me that there was probably not a lot of stuff in the bag that they would want anyway, and they had already taken some things in the days after the funeral. I had to let it go.

Mary wrote:

My Dan was a very blue-collar guy. He loved to dress up, but was more at home in his Levis and work shirts. His closet was never full as he only bought what he needed. When something wore out, it became a rag and was replaced with the same thing or something as similar as we could find.

We had shopped at Sears, of course, on December 18, his 53rd birthday. He was taking a work-related trip right after Christmas *vacation and wanted to look nice. We bought a couple pairs of jeans, a few nice dressy shirts and a jacket that he really liked. I remember his smile as he came out of the dressing room, rocking his new jacket. He never got to wear any of these clothes for his business trip. The tags were still in place.*

I went back to Sears a few weeks after the funeral with receipts in hand and when asked the reason for return, I burst into tears and related my story. The poor salesman was beside himself and of course quickly made the transaction.

The remainder of his wardrobe hung in the closet for over a year. This was a topic brought up in grief group and of course was such a different process for everyone. I remember spending time lingering in Dan's side of the closet and loving the feel and smell of his leather jacket, which I to this day have and continue to touch and smell.

Father Schuniki of the Capuchins (an order of priests that are loved and very present in Dan's hometown) collects clothes for the Samaritan House. I eventually donated Dan's clothes to that cause. I felt Dan would have been pleased with that decision.

Rhonda shared her experience:

Mike had given a lot of his personal items away while he was still alive...things he specifically wanted someone to have.

We had put a contract on a place before he passed, but closed after he passed. I was living in the apartment where he passed and couldn't bring myself to move into the new place. The main reason is I didn't want to go through the rest of Mike's stuff. After paying a mortgage and rent for a couple months, Mike's brother suggested I just pack all his stuff and move it with me to the new place. Once he suggested that, I felt much better to leave. So I packed it all up and moved to the new place. Over the next six months to a year I slowly got rid of stuff, either giving items to someone, or just to Goodwill, depending on what it was. I kept a few things…my favorite shirt we bought in Italy, his work boots and uniforms, his aviator sunglasses (which are on my bookshelf), wallet, daytimer. It was emotional every time I let go of something. It would bring back memories…some smiling and some crying with those memories.

Debbie's experience of dealing with Brant's personal effects:

I finally felt it was time to donate Brant's clothes after about one and a half years. As he had been a very successful businessman, I wanted to find a good home for his expensive suits, sports coats, etc. I searched online and found Denver Works, sort of the men's equivalent of Dress for Success. Denver Works helps men with the interview process and placement in the job force. I needed to set up an appointment for the donation process, which ended up being on our 36th wedding anniversary. My friend from work was supposed to go with me, but had to cancel last minute. I was absolutely dreading this, but it wasn't as bad as what I had anticipated. Still, crying on the way home, I needed a coffee and when I pulled into the usually very busy garage of the Starbucks in Cherry Creek, there was a parking space front and center. I took it as a sign from Brant that I had done the right thing.

Brant had been known for his expensive and beautiful tie collection. Both kids asked that I not donate the "best" ones. I was going to divide them up between the two kids, but ended up giving them to Jason *when he started his new job. Because of Brant's tie collection and love of Burberry, Jamie and Rick had Burberry ties at their wedding. The ties were Rick's gifts to his groomsmen.*

. 18 .
TAKING OFF THE RING

For the first few months, the topic of wedding rings did not come up. Then hesitantly one session someone wondered out loud how long we would continue to wear our rings. It was shocking at first to think about it.

But as one woman said, "I don't feel married anymore." Another said, "Every time I look down at my ring, it just makes me sad."

Many of us decided that the one-year anniversary would probably be the time that we would consider taking off the ring. For me, that would be March 17, 2009. Every month for the first year, the 17th was a significant day, so it was not unusual to mark that day.

When I decided on the day that I would remove the ring, I wanted to make a ceremony of it. I thought about what it would feel like all day long. That evening, I poured a glass of wine, a Côte du Rhône, Terry's favorite, and turned on some music: Bob Seger's "Against the Wind." We had been at a Seger concert in the last year, and this song was especially meaningful to us.

Well those drifter's days are past me now
I've got so much more to think about
Deadlines and commitments
What to leave in, what to leave out

Against the wind
I'm still runnin' against the wind
I'm older now but still runnin' against the wind
Well I'm older now and still runnin'
Against the wind

As the haunting melody played, I slowly removed the wedding ring I had worn for 33 years and gently placed it in its velvet box. By this time I was sobbing, and I let myself feel all the emotions I was blessed to feel.

Mary shares her thought about the wedding ring:

It's there. You just have to look a little closer, the indentation on the ring finger on the left hand. It seems to be fading away as the years go by, but I will always see it. It reminds me daily of the ring I wore for 30 years. The ring I was wearing on that fateful night over 10 years ago was not the original one I received on our wedding day. I had lost the diamond from the original ring at school and could not find it even though I tried. Dan was adamant that we return to the Shane Company where we bought the original one, and pick out a new ring. He did not want to just replace the diamond that was lost. He took such delight in picking out a new one.

When we discussed the wedding ring at group, there were a lot of great points brought up defending the case for wearing and for taking it off. It was over a year when I finally decided to take it off and put it in a safe place. I have kept the old band also. They are still there. They will always be a reminder of my marriage and my love for Dan.

From Debbie:

I remember there was a discussion at hospice about this, when all of us had joined the "club that no one wanted to join." I know I wasn't feeling married anymore, but didn't really know what to do. When I got home from the session and Applebee's, I did some research on the internet. There were no real clear guidelines online, but the general consensus seemed to be to move the ring to the right hand. I went to a jeweler to have my ring resized for my right hand. In the Jewish religion, the wedding ring is put on the right hand index finger, as it was believed there was a vein that ran from the index finger to the heart. That was where I wanted my ring to be. After wearing it on my right index finger, which was uncomfortable, I moved it to the right hand middle finger. After getting involved with Don, I took it off, except to wear at Jamie's wedding. My ring is now with Brant's in one of my bedroom drawers. Not a very safe location, but they're together.

From Rhonda:

I honestly can't remember exactly when I quit wearing my wedding ring but I remember it being traumatic. I know it was a couple years and was a difficult decision. I would take it off a few days and then put it back on. I wore Mike's wedding ring on a necklace chain for several *years. Lindsay got married several years after I had not been wearing my ring. I put it on the day of the wedding. It was not something I contemplated. I just put it on that day because it felt right.*

Janet had her rings and Dave's melded together into one new ring she designed. She now wears the blended ring on her right hand. It is beautiful. My wedding ring is in my safe deposit box, waiting for the day that one of the granddaughters might want to have it reset. I have enough jewelry from Terry for each granddaughter to eventually have a piece.

Recently my cousin Larry lost his wife to early Alzheimer's disease. He felt comfortable asking me about taking off the ring. "When would it be appropriate? It just reminds me every time I look at it that I am no longer married to Carla." I assured him that the decision is personal, and that he could do whatever felt best for him. It might seem like such an insignificant thing to someone who has not had that loss. But removing a tangible sign of the relationship that many of us had for decades has a profound effect on us.

· 19 ·
MOVING FORWARD

"The reality is that you will grieve forever. You will not 'get over' the loss of a loved one; you will learn to live with it. You will heal and you will rebuild yourself around the loss you have suffered. You will be whole again, but you will never be the same. Nor should you be the same, nor would you want to."
ELIZABETH KUBLER-ROSS AND DAVID KESSLER

THERE WERE TIMES THAT I FELT I could never, ever get over my loss. When I finally accepted that I was not supposed to "get over it," it was easier to move forward.

With a profound loss, you have the need to grieve, but also the need to live at the same time. We discussed many times that moving forward meant not burying ourselves with our spouses, but honoring them by living life and learning to enjoy life once more.

New purchases that we made for the first time without our spouses were difficult. When Karen proudly bought her first new car after Damian died, she was parking it on a street near Sue's house where we were having dinner. A man looked at the car with envy and said, "What did you have to do to get a car like that?" Karen replied without thinking, "Bury my husband." The conversation ended abruptly.

It's not easy, nor should it be. There are some practical things we did to work through this stage of our grief. Our sessions at the hospice support group moved us forward to accept the reality of our loss as one of our first tasks. Until that happened, I could not move forward. Eventually, I was able to remove Terry's shoes from the front door, then remove his clothes from the closet. Eventually, I could go to bed at night without falling asleep crying, or waking up in the middle of the night, pleading, wondering, "Where did you go?" Accepting the loss is one of the main tasks of grieving.

It helped to know that others were going through the same process and to listen to their stories. In the group, we always had permission to fully experience the pain of our grief. We knew no one in that group was there to judge. We talked about what it was like moving around furniture in your house without having to consult anyone, because now it is *your* house. Even the seemingly small move of looking at your spouse's favorite coffee cup and deciding to move it to another shelf brought empathetic nods of understanding. We learned that, until we had fully gone through the numerous kinds of pain in grief, we could not move forward.

Granted there were times during the sessions when people were clearly not in the same place in their grieving process as others. As time went on and other people joined the group, we had to go through the same beginning steps with them.

One particularly wrenching session happened when several of us who had been in the group for close to two years were wondering if it could ever happen again: Could we be ready for other relationships? A new attendee was so offended by this topic that she could not accept we were even talking about this.

We understood, but it was also evident from this episode that it was time for some of us to "graduate" from the group. The hospice worker (it was not Sarah anymore, as she had a new baby and was not working with the evening group now) suggested delicately that perhaps we needed to make room for newly bereaved people. A lifelong bond of friendship and love had formed during those two years of support group attendance at the hospice. We had progressed well in the group, but as the hospice worker noted, it might be time for us to leave. We agreed.

The hospice wisely let us know it was time to exit the Younger Bereaved Spouses support group and get going on the other tasks of grief: adjusting to our changed situations, at work, at home, and in society in general.

A group of us continued to meet often, those first few years. At first, it was a larger group—including some men we dearly loved—who met monthly to continue our process. As we adjusted to our new status in the world, we could then start to reinvest in new relationships and life in general. For me, talking about it and listening to others led to the path to resilience. Journaling and reading books about grief were helpful in maneuvering toward resilience.

After a while eight of us women formed our own group, no longer strictly a grief group, but a sisterhood. We were the "Sister Chicks," or "Sistahs," Janet's term for us as we all hated the word "widow." We would meet almost weekly at first, at happy hours, at dinners at each other's homes, and traveling.

Since all of us had trouble with cooking in those first years, we became accustomed to ordering appetizers everywhere we went. Four of the girls went to Las Vegas for a first getaway and ate nothing but appetizers the whole time. I think it was just too painful to cook for one at first. I never did really get used to it.

We started having monthly dinners at each other's places. Jan was a big promoter of this activity. She would write to all of us and then suggested we start taking turns doing the dinners. She would make us "sign up" so the months wouldn't pass without a dinner. Those early dinners were godsends to us, as we no longer had the every-other-week sessions at the hospice to check out if what we were feeling was normal. The happy hours were more spontaneous, but the dinners were a sacred ritual. We eventually got over our "appetizers only" mindset and our dinners together at each other's house were anything from pizza and salad to Karen's gourmet creations.

This was a group where you could admit that you still slept in your husband's T-shirts, that you still had not erased his voice from your answering machine, and that you were feeling some relief that you no longer were in charge of the caretaking.

Following in the tradition of the Denver Hospice, we crafted our own list of ways to cope. Our widow's humor came through as we paraphrased some of the suggestions from the original list we read at our first meeting.

We added:

"Be present as fully as possible. Two or more absences from happy hour will be discussed in the group."

"Silence? What's that? It is NOT a member of this group!"

"Observe deep confidentiality unless consuming vast quantities of wine, and then anyone is a target, especially if they didn't show up that time."

Along the way, we experienced some "pivot points" that showed us maybe we were coming out of deep grief, and that we had survived. When we no longer felt the need to count the days or hours until our next group session; when we found ourselves musing over possible new relationships; when we could talk about our spouses without pausing to wipe tears; when we could conjure up more good memories than sorrowful ones—these were the signs to us and to our group facilitator that we were ready to move beyond the group for further healing.

Many of us hated the expression "moving on" after the loss. To us that inferred people thought we had just moved on with no more thought to what we had lost and what we had been through, but that we just wanted to forget the sadness and the past. Nothing could be further from the truth. You never "get over it." But to me, if I wanted to honor the memory of Terry, the most positive thing I could do was to *"move forward," to embrace life, to find joy, and to learn to live again.*

Moving us out of the group was the last gift the hospice gave us. We were ready to strike out on our own, to develop a new self-identity based on a life without the person who left too soon. I was ready to find out who I was separate from my role as Terry's spouse. I had to figure out who I really was without Terry.

Not "moving on," just moving forward the best way I knew how.

. 20 .
WIDOWS GONE WILD

*"We must be willing to let go of the life we planned
so as to have the life that is waiting for us."*
JOSEPH CAMPBELL

A YEAR OR SO AFTER OUR GROUP had graduated from the Younger Bereaved Spouses support group, six of us decided to take a trip together to Mexico. (Karen and Sue had previous commitments and could not go.) We had no idea when we started making plans and dreaming about our tropical vacation together how much that trip would change our lives.

When we arrived at our hotel in Playa del Carmen, Janet picked up a brochure at the lobby's activity desk. The colorful pamphlet advertised an excursion called Tulum Extreme. It included zip lining and rappelling and *cenote* swimming—activities none of us had ever done. In fact, we'd never dreamed of doing such things. Janet talked us into signing up.

Some among us are more adventurous than others, but we all had a bit of trepidation about what we had signed up for. Jan was probably the most enthusiastic.

On the day of the excursion we gathered in the lobby, not knowing what to expect. Off we went on the bus with our guide, Marcel, who was a delight. "My friends…" he would begin every activity.

The first stop was for rappelling.

The Mexican sun beat down on us as we made our way up the mountain with Marcel. I had a heaviness in the pit of my stomach. It was simply not like me to embark on an adventure like this. We kept wondering what our spouses would have said about it, and agreed most of them would have said it was out of character.

Rappelling is the act of lowering yourself on a controlled descent down the side of a cliff dangling from a rope. It was striking to me that one of the most important things you can do in this activity is to lean back and trust the ropes are strong enough for you to make your way down the mountain.

Jan was the first to go. As I watched her confidently begin her rappelling, (Jan has always seemed a bit more daring than the rest of us), I was so touched by her ability to just lean back and go with the flow. The rest of us were not so eager. We stood and watched, begging someone else to go next. Eventually one at a time, we were all able to muster the courage to scale the cliff.

As it became my turn, I dangled on the rope suspended between cliff and thin air, and stared at the distant ground (against the advice of Marcel). Thoughts raced through my head. *What in the hell am I doing here? What if I don't make it down? Am I strong enough to hold onto this rough rope?* and finally *Who will tell the kids if I don't make it?*

I am not a very adventurous person; I don't even go on carnival rides. And here I was, wearing a rock-climbing helmet, strapped into a harness that was wrapped around my midsection and attached to a bright red rope hanging 60 feet over the edge of a mountain. Little by little, I inched my way down the side of the cliff. The rope swayed slightly with each movement, and occasionally I felt a minor jerk in the line as my weight adjusted to the descent. I'd hold my breath, then release it as I followed Marcel's instructions to push my feet off the mountainside, gradually, slowly, lowering myself closer to the ground. When my feet at last safely hit the ground, I felt a new sense of strength.

I could do it!

To allow myself to be lowered off that cliff took me out of my comfort zone and forced me to trust in something completely out of my control. This step became a sign to me—that I was ready to move forward with the next part of my life, and when I choose to really live, I honor the memory of Terry so much more than if I just comfortably lived the rest of my life without taking any chances.

Zip lining was next. Marcel made sure we wore our heavy gloves as he safely strapped us one at a time to the zip line cord. While we were lining up to zip line, waiting our turn, we would chat with Marcel as he got us ready to go. He wanted to know why we were traveling together, and we told him our story. We always seemed to have a need to tell our story to random strangers whom we perceived would be sympathetic and interested. (Later we became tired of that, and Mary recalls Deb telling people they golfed with, wearing a very serious face, that they met as table dancers at Shotgun Willies. Mary said it was pretty funny as looks of sympathy were replaced with looks of shock. Widow's humor.)

I stepped onto the platform and gazed out at the expansive view in front of me. The zip line extended almost a half mile, with the other end of the cable disappearing into the Mayan jungle. I felt dizzy as I looked down at the trees, a distant 70 feet below me. Marcel didn't give me time to change my mind and gave me a nudge to take off.

As I pushed off on the zip line cord, grasping tightly with my hands encased in the heavy gloves, my first thought was, *Oh God, what have I done now?* By this time, I had seven grandchildren, and I wondered what would happen if I never saw them again.

But after about forty seconds of these kinds of thoughts, I started to enjoy myself. I purposed myself to try to be in the moment, looking down at the treetops. The fresh air hit my face, and I felt like I was flying. The wind whipped my hair as I allowed myself to feel the freedom of soaring through the tropical jungle.

I experienced a feeling of letting go I had never felt before. Nothing I'd ever done previously in my life equaled this new exhilarating feeling of letting go. I was letting go of my concerns, my trepidation, my fears, the darkness of my grief. This dramatic moment altered my life. Zipping through the air I felt a new boldness, a new determination, a new confidence.

I felt resilient!

I have pictures of all of us as we sped across the zip line, and most of us actually let go of the cord during our zip line experience. This courageous act was symbolic of our willingness to let go of our other life and embrace the new with elation.

Our final activity was *cenote*, or underground cave swimming. These subterranean swimming holes hold special meaning for the Mayan people. In ancient times the Mayan saw *cenotes* as sacred, often a place for sacrificial offerings. That day, the refreshing waters held similar meaning for us.

We had been wearing swimsuits under our rappelling clothes, so we could easily remove our outer layer of clothing and climb into the *cenote* with Marcel. The fresh, cool water seemed like a welcome relief after the grueling heat of the Mexican sun. We lazily swam around the cave until we heard Mary say in a soft pleading voice, "Um, you guys, I can't swim." This little detail had escaped her memory until that moment. Marcel had to rescue her for the rest of the swimming experience, which led us to believe perhaps she had not forgotten she couldn't swim, but waited until that moment to tell us. In either case, we swam and floated in the cooling waters, leaving our cares behind. We reveled in the sacred waters and our newfound freedom.

Later that day when we returned to our rooms, I noticed the Tulum Extreme pamphlet on the table. The subtitle on the ad read "Over the Edge." Indeed. Over the edge of fear. Over the edge of expectations others had for us. Over the edge of the darkest part of our grief and coming out on the other side.

The trip was a monumental turning point for all six of us. We had spent a harrowing day doing activities that most of us would never have attempted in our former lives. (Meanwhile, Jan begged the guides to let her do it all again, and I have not done any of those things since.) Each one of us threw caution to the wind and embraced the Tulum Extreme adventure. And as a result, we each gained a new freedom. Each of us learned we could be resilient and survive this difficult life transition. We literally discovered new heights, gained a greater sense of self-worth, and started to feel a heightened appreciation of life. We talked again about what we thought the reactions of our spouses would be to this event. Most felt our spouses would never have gone for this adventure. At one point, after one of the longest and most terrifying zip lines, we stood on the top of one of the final towers. Debbie gazed at the cliffs below us and remarked, "Look at us! We are the Widows Gone Wild!"

And so, from that day, we were the Widows Gone Wild, the WGW.

For the rest of our Mexico trip, we had long, lazy afternoons where we could sit on the beach and pour out our hearts about moving forward from our losses, and exploring our hopes for carrying on.

On the final evening of our adventure, we went to a dance club after a nice dinner in Playa. We donned our cute summer dresses, smoothed aloe on our sunburns, and headed to the dance club after dinner. It felt a little odd to us to be doing this, as most of us had not done a lot of this kind of activity since our spouses died. Of course, we were there much earlier than the locals, who wouldn't arrive until after we were long gone. We told the DJ that we would like some of "our music" in addition to the techno music he would be playing. We were dancing and having a good time, when suddenly in the middle of a techno song came a line from John Mellencamp's "Jack and Diane." The DJ had inserted it for us.

Oh yeah, life goes on. Long after the thrill of living is gone.

The WGW all looked at each other knowingly and continued to dance, confident that, indeed, life was going on for us.

· 21 ·
REINVESTING IN LIFE

"Doesn't everything die, and too soon? Tell me, what is it you plan to do with your one wild and precious life?"
POET MARY OLIVER

I STILL MARVEL AT THE TRANSFORMATION, from sad-eyed widows to back-to-vibrant women. Grief is a fine teacher of resilience.

Working through grief, if you are willing to do the work, can make you come out on the other side as a stronger more resilient person than you ever believed possible. I could see this happening in my fellow WGW.

The road to resilience, however, is not an easy one. In the support group, we were encouraged to realize that our spouse's death was not an insurmountable problem, but also to realize that it would take time. We received quite a bit of information so that we could recognize the subtle ways that we were getting better. We began to accept that loss is an inherent part of life, and we were not alone in our grief. We started to find pleasure again in the activities of life that we had enjoyed before and to add new ones. Our travels together gave us the opportunity to discover new parts of ourselves and to appreciate life more than ever. Several of us, (but not all of us on all the trips), went on a few trips together—Las Vegas, Florida, Italy, a dance cruise, and our trip to Mexico—all a big part of our healing process.

We also learned that grief is a very personal experience, and while we benefitted greatly from talking with each other and experiencing new activities, each of us had to learn to identify the ways that would work for us and to incorporate those into our individual lives.

When we accepted that we were never going to return to our former selves, we became intent on defining our newly formed selves. Being in a group that supported this made a huge difference in getting stronger and resilient.

We shared small victories, the first new car in the group, the first time someone fixed a faucet alone, taking out a mortgage in your own name, all experiences that buoyed us and moved us forward. For some selling our houses or renovating so that it became a reflection of ours alone was important. We were grateful every time we had to do something to adjust to our new life situation; having the courage to try some online dating, "dinner with friends," and joining a dance group. There were many opportunities for self-discovery and we took as many as we could.

One WGW had an unexpected turn of events when she found herself developing feelings for a woman, which was a completely new experience. Although the "crush" never became more than just that, it launched her into a period of self-discovery and open mindedness. Eleven months later, much of which were spent in therapy, she allowed herself to not label what love is supposed to look like. She met a woman with whom she has shared a beautiful and long-term relationship, and is thankful to have experienced such a love.

Our new appreciation for life led many of us to discover a new courage, a new sense of strength, and finally, resilience.

Grief, though it did not disappear entirely, became less a force in our lives than the courage to function independently. Grief began to dissipate and life to return. It does not happen to everyone in the same time period, but I found by giving myself permission to grieve deeply, I could also give myself permission to let it run its course and then begin to laugh and love again. I have "one wild and precious life," and I did not want to spend it being sad all the time. That is definitely a sign of resilience: the capacity to live a full life without guilt or regret.

Even now eleven years later, I have pangs of sadness, moments of deep longing, but they are less frequent and less intense, and I am grateful every day for my resilience.

. 22 .
TIME DOES HEAL, WITH HELP

WE OFTEN HEAR THE EXPRESSION, "Time heals all wounds." Many bereaved people have a hard time believing that statement. When you are immersed in your grief, it feels like your whole world has stopped and you can't imagine it ever going on again. As I think back on my own experience of healing, I know the sorrow can be replaced by cherished memories and you can move forward with your life after great loss. I am speaking from the perspective of the loss of a spouse. That is my experience.

But time alone does not heal.

If individuals who lose a loved one are unable to move through the acceptance of their loss and the adjustment of her new reality more than a year after the loss, they can be said to be suffering from complicated, or prolonged, grief. There has been an improved focus on complicated grief in the past few years, now that we know there is no real timeline for the "stages" of grief.

At first, the symptoms of normal grief are similar to those of complicated grief: the deep sorrow, the difficulty accepting one's new reality, the pain of adjustment to life alone. For most people, the shock of the loss and the intense feelings of grief gradually subside; within a year they regain resilience and are able to function effectively. They can go about their daily lives without much disruption.

For others, the feelings of grief do not ease and do not improve even after a long time passes. Sometimes the symptoms worsen. In prolonged grief, painful emotions are so severe and persistent that a person has a difficult time recovering. Some may find it practically impossible to resume the daily life they had before the loss. The severe sadness, which is helpful in the early grief process, becomes debilitating if it continues without end. Prolonged grief paralyzes resilience. It keeps the grieving person in a hopeless state of lingering grief. I know of two widows with complicated grief who are still suffering years after their loss. There is such a difference between normal grief and prolonged grief.

For those suffering from prolonged grief, I urge you to seek help. Friends and family can be your most faithful comforters, but even their tolerance and patience is not without limit. Look for a professional bereavement counselor, who will allow you the freedom to express your honest emotions and who can guide you towards healing. Several members of our grief support group sought out individual counseling in addition to the group support. Many said they could not possibly have attended group without doing some individual work first. Also, you may find healing support in your church community.

Regardless which stage of grief you find yourself in, consider joining a bereavement group. In our grief group at the hospice, we were able to come to an acceptance of our new reality together as we shared stories and anxieties. We were able to experience the pain of our loss together. We were able to eventually talk about renewed interest and purpose in life and for some, new relationships.

This I know to be true: Without the support of the hospice and the Younger Bereaved Spouses support group, and then the WGW, I would have had a much more difficult time completing my journey to resilience. I would not have healed as well if I had not acted on my own part. The world can only take so much of sympathizing with you. I found joining the hospice support group was the single most profound action I took toward my own healing in the two years following Terry's death.

One dictionary defines resilience as the ability to become healthier, happy, or strong again after a problem. When do you turn the corner from grief to comfort, from sadness to acceptance, from crying at every memory to smiling that it happened? It does not happen automatically or quickly. In the illustrated children's book, *Tear Soup*, that many of us found so helpful through the years, the authors wrote that Grandy, the main character, was finally able to quit cooking the tear soup and could put the rest of it in the freezer and just take out a little "or a taste" once in a while. I found this to be true, and still do years later. I am able to go back to old memories on holidays and anniversaries, linger with them a bit and then return to my current day, comforted that I have not forgotten, but have found unexpected new ways to move forward.

I could continue to lead my travel groups. I could hire someone to do my taxes without freaking out. My teaching job no longer seemed daunting like it did in those first months when I had to convince myself to get out of bed every morning.

I have found the jigsaw puzzle of my life has changed and the old pieces no longer fit, and I shouldn't keep trying to fit them back in the old places. I have learned to turn the new pieces over carefully and find the new me I was becoming. Happiness did not find me again: I made it happen.

I decided I would not be bitter that the picture of my life would never be the same. I could fit the new pieces in and marvel at the new life that I was living.

. 23 .
A NEW WAY TO MARK TIME

As we moved forward during the weeks and then months of our grief journey in the hospice group and then later with the WGW, I noticed a tendency for all of us to mark time in a very different way from anything we had ever done. For the first year, the 17th of each month (Terry had died on March 17), I was reminded that my life had changed irreversibly.

In the group, we would share those stark reminders with one another. Since we met two times per month, it was not unusual for our meeting date to coincide with someone's loved one's death anniversary and even, for some of us, the date that our spouse was diagnosed with the dreaded disease. In the group, we always started the sessions by lighting a candle and saying our spouse's cause of death and his date of death. Each time someone would remark that it was "exactly" so many months since the spouse died, there were murmurings of comfort and empathy around the table. When I look back, I remember how deeply those dates affected me. It has helped me to empathize with the newly widowed people I have met, to remember the markings of those days.

Of course, when the year anniversaries rolled around, it was yet more poignant. Many of us would plan to do something special or just "get out of town" when the anniversary dates rolled around. For instance, since Mary's husband died on December 27, just a couple of days after Christmas, she had a yearly ritual of going with her family on a cruise during that time. Hers was a sudden loss, and she just couldn't bear being around on Christmas.

Mary shares:

It does not seem possible that it has been eleven years, during the Christmas season, that I lost the man I love. At the time, I believed it would not be possible to enjoy the holiday season and tried to avoid the sorrow I remembered on that day. I traveled each year for the first five or so years and tried to create new and happier memories. It seemed to be a short "fix," but eventually I decided to face the holidays at home.

The pain is still there and I reflect on, especially at this festive time of year, my 30+ years of marriage and that fateful night in December. However, with the love and support of my God, my family and close "widow" friends, I have managed to survive and begin new traditions. He will always be a part of our lives; as a matter of fact, my youngest son posted a picture of him on his anniversary and gave a wonderful tribute to his dad. Many friends who knew him echoed his accomplishments. Our loved ones do not have to be forgotten, but remembered and celebrated.

When asked for advice on how to "move past" such a devastating event, it remains difficult for me to give advice. I share how it affected me and what skills I used to cope with the trauma, but other than that I do not feel I am capable to give advice. Everyone has to find their own ways to cope, to remember, and to heal.

Since I had a large family with several grandchildren (I now have nine), it was more meaningful to me to spend time with them at my home on the anniversary date. For the first couple of years, the grandchildren released balloons "up to heaven," until we became more ecologically aware and stopped doing that. For ten years, St. Patrick's Day had been such a sad day for me, the day Terry died in 2008. Thank God I am not Irish and have never had much of a desire to celebrate St. Patrick's Day, because that would make the day even harder to bear. As it is, I couldn't bear that day and the celebrations that come with it.

Early in March during those years, I would start to feel a somewhat free-floating sadness and anxiety, and then one day, I would wake up and remember why. The day was approaching. Since Terry's birthday was also in March, that feeling kind of took over the whole month. During the years that Easter fell in March, it was kind of a triple whammy, since Terry had died during Holy Week and his funeral was the day after Easter. For years, even now, when the date approaches to mark the anniversary of my loss, if I have forgotten a little about it, suddenly for days, I feel off-kilter, like something is wrong, and I can't put my finger on it. Then I glance at the calendar and say, "Oh that's it. It's almost the anniversary date."

Things changed on the tenth anniversary, however. I was spending the winter in Florida and had decided long before that I would make the trip back to Colorado to commemorate the tenth anniversary of Terry's death with my kids and grandkids. I told the WGW about my plans, and they were interested in what I had envisioned for the day. I planned the day carefully. I would go to the cemetery alone in the morning, and the kids and their families would arrive for lunch later.

I prepared a true St. Patrick's Day meal, something I had not done for ten years, corned beef and cabbage, the works. I dug out the slide show that was used for Terry's funeral with pictures of his childhood that the grandkids had never seen. I watched it by myself first to make sure that I would not dissolve into a puddle of tears while the kids were watching it.

And I resurrected an earlier tradition: The grandkids would release balloons from the back deck like we used to do on the anniversary. I wanted the younger grandkids to participate, as they had never had the chance. I told them to call out their names as they each released a balloon separately. How touching it was to hear the sound of their little voices calling up to a grandfather that most had never met. "Adam! Viola! Iris! Hannah! Matthew! Michael! Audrey! Emma!" Standing on our back deck and hearing those names echo through the air as the balloons floated heavenward, I couldn't help but believe that somewhere, Terry was hearing these sweet voices of his grandchildren, most of whom he had never gotten to meet. As the oldest "Alyssa!" called out her name and her balloon went sailing, there was a resounding echo. I like to think the intended recipient was watching and sending his love back.

After year ten, I told myself I would not let St. Patrick's Day bother me anymore. That did not really work for me. Having just recently observed the eleventh anniversary of Terry's death, I found it is just not possible for me to ignore the calendar. When I related to my sister Karen that I was still hating St. Patrick's Day as much as ever, she reassured me, "Maybe it's okay if that date is always bothersome. Life is not as tidy as we'd like."

After the first year anniversary, most of us quit marking the day every month, but all of us still remember and mark the anniversary date. Many in the group still commemorate the date of the loss by withdrawing and spending the day "inside yourself" thinking about the loved one gone forever, but also reflecting on the astounding way that time has of flying by and about how far we have come since that time.

In his book, *The Other Side of Sadness*, George Bonanno writes of "anniversary reactions" in which the bereaved person experiences "a dramatic increase in sadness or loneliness on the anniversary of an important date related to the loss." Birthdays, special holidays, wedding anniversaries, and of course the date of death of the loved one, all are days when these reactions are triggered. Over time, Bonnano says the duration does not change much, but the frequency of the reactions does. For me the duration of my anniversary reactions has lessened dramatically. The flame flickers, but it never goes out completely.

Sue shared her musings on John's anniversary date:
Sitting on my beautiful deck tonight thinking about eleven years

ago. We were getting ready to say goodbye to a remarkable man, Johnny W. Kafer. It is so hard to believe that he has been gone eleven years. We miss him still. We have remarkable memories, and we learned it is important to say goodbye with no guilt and no regret; we thank him for that. He died with such dignity. Hey babe, we love you to this day.

Rhonda shared:

I was snowshoeing at Winter Park on January 14, 2017, the exact ten-year anniversary of Mike's passing. As we were making our way through the beautiful, peaceful mountainside a helicopter flew over. (Mike had been a helicopter pilot). It made my heart feel good. I laid in the snow and made a snow angel and wrote I love you.

· 24 ·
KEEPING TRADITIONS ALIVE

"Tradition is tending the flame, not worshipping the ashes."
COMPOSER GUSTAV MAHLER

DURING THE FIRST YEAR after the loss, on every holiday, I reflected on last year at this time. *Terry was still here.* I used to think that after the first year of holidays without my beloved, it would be easier. It is not a lot easier, but at least I could remind myself I survived a whole year.

With time all of the WGW came to the conclusion we could celebrate holidays as usual, avoid the holidays altogether, or start new traditions. We get to decide. In the beginning, truth be told, there are no great alternatives. For every grieving family, the holidays will come and go and they will have survived another difficult occasion.

It helped us to start new traditions when we could. Several of the WGW no longer repeat old traditions from their previous lives. It somehow seemed a bit easier to start new ones.

The arrival of seven additional grandchildren in the few years after Terry died assured my family that holidays would be changing. I was still occasionally blindsided by a rush of emotions during the Christmas and Easter holidays. It helped if I did not suppress the emotions, because if I did, they would resurface again and again. If I dealt with them in the moment and allowed myself to grieve, the feelings would eventually go away and allow me to make changes.

There are some survival strategies that worked for me and the group. I found the world would not end if I didn't prepare for holidays with the energy or enthusiasm of previous years.

As time went on, I started to relax a little about being afraid I was going to forget Terry. We had so many years together and so many traditions it seemed every month and season brought precious memories that eventually made me smile rather than cry.

The first Christmas after Terry died, Joel announced ahead of time that he would carry on the Christmas Eve tradition of making oyster stew, a favorite activity of his dad's. I did not anticipate the emotions that washed over me when he walked in my door that Christmas Eve with his stew-making supplies. I came completely unglued and had to leave the room for a bit. No one noticed until my daughter-in-law, Ellen, realized I was not saying much and couldn't eat the soup. She gently asked how I was doing on this first Christmas. I can assuredly say that in the intervening Christmases, as Joel has added to his recipe and made the stew his own concoction, it has become a comforting ritual and a way to remember Terry and his love of food.

Another Christmas tradition is my over-the-years Christmas photo album. I had always kept a separate beautiful photo album of pictures from the Christmases of our 33-year marriage. In 2008, the year of Terry's death, I stopped placing pictures in that album, but I still bring it out on Christmas Eve, and the kids love to go through it. They remember the Christmases when their dad was healthy, laughing at the old pictures and remembering those early times of their lives. It is not a sad activity, but one with moments of hilarity and fond stories. It does not damper the holiday spirit one bit, but gives the assurance that their dad is not forgotten.

We kept up the tradition for several years of releasing balloons on the anniversary of Terry's death, March 17. They were always white balloons at first, as Terry used to tease his twin granddaughters that white was his favorite color. They thought this was hilarious. When we brought back the balloon tradition on the tenth anniversary, we added green balloons to the white collection.

The WGW all agree that remembering our late spouses in words and actions is a big part of healing and consolation. Whether we keep old traditions, or create new ones, we are honoring the memories of our loved ones by embracing holidays and life fully. We are not "worshipping the ashes" of our departed spouses, but "tending the flame."

Mary wrote about her sons going hunting together in November:
I love when they get together to do this as Dan was big on hunting, and I feel he would be so happy they are keeping his tradition alive.

· 25 ·
SACRED SPACE

As TIME WENT ON, many of us were faced with the fear that we would lose connection with our loved ones. Many of us kept pictures, belongings, and mementos around the house. But for some of us, these reminders had a way of making us feel "stuck."

We were lucky to be part of the hospice program that would continue to send out "Healing Hearts," a monthly newsletter for the recently bereaved. In one of those monthly letters, it was suggested that you could continue your connection with loved ones by creating a space in your home to gather physical evidence of the existence of your lost loved one. This was an enormous help to me. It gave me permission to contain memories of Terry, yet to move ahead with life and to re-enter the world.

My sacred space is a nook in the family room in my basement. There are three shelves where I have placed photos of me and Terry at various times of our marriage; our wedding day, pictures of us with our children as infants and young children, photos of Terry and me as empty nesters on traveling adventures. I know I can visit that space whenever I wish and feel close to Terry once more. With this sacred space, I can feel the presence of Terry when I stand in front of that nook, look at the pictures and remember where and when they were taken. It gives me great solace.

I have since remarried, to a widower whose wife of 34 years died one year before Terry. Jeff also has a sacred space in that same room, an alcove with three shelves as well. We welcome the memories that these spaces evoke. The connections we have with each other are very different from the ones we had with our first spouses. We tell each other stories of our first marriages, remember birthdays and anniversaries, and are okay with knowing that this relationship does not diminish what we had before.

Janet wrote:

I guess it's a sacred place although I don't remember when or why I did this. I have a picture of Dave (actually it is the card from his memorial service with his picture on the front) stuck inside a plant that someone gave me at the time of his death. Amazingly enough, I have been able to keep it alive all this time. It is in my office in front of my desk so I see it every day. I have to turn the plant to get even light from the window, and so I have to turn the picture so he's facing me all the time.

Rhonda shared:

Without much thought, I immediately had two photos of Mike on the shelves in the living room. Along with a statue of a bride and groom we received at our wedding, a copy of his dog tags, his aviator glasses, and a stone he used for potential healing powers after he was diagnosed with cancer. Have since added a key to a lock Lindsay and I left in Italy on a bridge, and a picture of just Mike. Just in the last few months I moved the pictures of the two of us to my bedroom.

Mary shared:

When Dan passed away in December, he left a void in my life as well as a void in the lives of his large German family in Kansas. He had such a presence while presiding over family events, such as carving the Thanksgiving turkey, making his favorite chicken fried steak, driving the combine for Harvest, or making his opinion known to all, that it only seemed fitting to honor his memory with a visible sign. At family gatherings it was so natural to devote a space to his memory. This began as simple as having his picture with a candle near a space such as an empty chair at the table, or displaying his favorite apron in the kitchen or a special hat of his hanging on the coat rack.

As the years ticked by, it was time to create a permanent space in a prominent but special resting spot. We had a wonderful picture taken on our vacation to Alaska the July before he passed. He was very relaxed on that trip and enjoyed the cruise around the glaciers, and his smile and body language depicted that. I wanted to see his picture before I retired for the evening to place a kiss on the lips I would not ever kiss again, so the bedroom seemed the logical place. I placed his picture with a beautiful ceramic candleholder given to me by a niece with a blessed candle inside. Our family is very spiritual and a candle is our way of gaining the attention of Our Lord. When I found a pair of his glasses in a drawer, they were placed near the picture and candle. A prayer card from his funeral also seemed appropriate. After ten years

I continue to keep that sacred space devoted to him. It was never a thought to put the picture away, or replace it with something else.

. 26 .
PATTERNS OF RESILIENCE

A FEW YEARS AGO, shortly after Terry died, I went to London for a convention. With a travel group, I toured many historic places including the last place where Queen Victoria had lived with her husband, Albert. The tour guide told us solemnly that Victoria never did get over her husband's death and pined for him for the rest of her life. "She loved him so much," he explained, "that she was not able to cope with him being gone." *Wow,* I thought to myself, *is there something wrong with me that I don't feel that way, that I just go on living and enjoying life? Did I not love Terry as much as Victoria loved Albert?*

Often people think that how much we grieve is indicative of how much we cared about the person we lost. This is simply not true. Few of us would want the people we left behind to grieve forever after we die. Our love is not measured by the way we grieve. It is a testament to our deceased loved one to keep growing, living, and wholeheartedly embracing life. To keep on living is a sign of resilience.

I observed several varying patterns of resilience in our small group. When I started writing this book and asked the WGW if they would consider answering some prompts for me so that I could include different experiences in the book, Karen asserted she felt no need to "revisit" that period of her life, but continually encourages me in my work and later graciously agreed to share her story. Sue recently wrote that, although she has many wonderful memories of her late husband John, whom she deeply loved, she has remarried and feels a need to no longer revisit those days after the loss, but rather to focus her time on her new life.

Sue says:
Life with John was a remarkable and wonderful 40 years. For some of the widows, it was new lives with travel and new adventures. For me, it was about once again raising tomatoes and squash.

I love that statement of Sue's. It reminds me of why I set out to write this memoir in the first place: I want to reassure the newly bereaved there is no wrong way to work through this formerly unthinkable life circumstance.

In her book, *The Gift of Years*, Sister Joan Chittister states: "Memory is a mental function, yes, but it is also a choice. We get to decide which of our memories of a particular time, or person, or place, or moment may shape our life in the present moment." Even in our group of eight, each of us has a different way of working through our memories day after day. The one constant is that hardly a day goes by we don't think of our deceased loved ones, but we honor their memory by moving forward in life and finding joy.

The WGW often noted after the first year, how quickly our conversations would change from sad reminisces of our late spouse to regular conversations about our lives, our kids, our attempts at dating, and other "normal" topics. Sometimes while driving home from the hospice support group, I was startled to realize I was no longer crying all the way home. Healing came in little spurts as we began to organize and plan for the future rather than being mired in our grief.

We also embraced the ability to laugh, even if our widow's humor may have seemed to some a bit morbid.

We teased Mary when she reported at one of our dinners she had noticed an attractive man at one of her archdiocesan gatherings at the cemetery where her husband was buried. We came up with a list of things they could say to get the conversation going: "So we have both had a loss. How about meeting at the cemetery stone to discuss this a bit more?" Or eventually just, "Meet you at the stone!" Or even, "Your stone or mine?" Mary reported she never got any further than a sympathetic nod and a, "How are you?" but thanked us for our suggestions anyway.

And dance. The WGW love wedding dances. We love dancing, and we love being happy. At Rhonda's daughter's wedding, the tables all had cards with the names of places that the couple had traveled to. Our table was Vancouver. Karen promptly changed it to read "Vancougars," more widow humor. At one wedding, the girls never stopped dancing, and at one point, a woman remarked, "You have such a great group. I'd love to join that club." We assured her it was a club she'd never want to have to qualify for.

· 27 ·
NOT REPLACING ANYBODY

AND THEN, THE TIME CAME for several of us to feel like we could date again and maybe even remarry. It's a very personal decision. For some, the period of the spouse's illness was so extended that there was time for preparing and for anticipatory grieving, the imagining of what it would be like after one's spouse is gone.

For me, that was a two-year period. Terry was diagnosed in February of 2006, and we had known since July of 2005 that something was very wrong that the doctors could not seem to find. He died in March of 2008. For over two years, we knew he was going to die from his disease, pancreatic cancer, once it was diagnosed. For a period of time, when he had started chemo, he seemed better and even gained some weight. One time our kids were having dinner with us and one of them expressed the hope that maybe he was going to get better after all. Terry looked at them, and said softly, "You know I am not going to survive this, right?" The room became very quiet, and one of them replied, "Yes."

For people who don't understand the concept of anticipatory grieving, they can't imagine that you can possibly be thinking of dating or moving forward before at least two years have passed. I had to learn to overlook thoughtless statements that people would make. Several married women commented on the thought of remarriage when I announced that Jeff and I were engaged, "Oh, I could never remarry. I just know I would not 'need' to do that again." As if they could possibly know what they would be feeling or needing under this circumstance. Although I have heard many women (who are not experiencing widowhood) say they could never, ever date or marry again, it is a completely personal decision and no one, absolutely no one, knows what she would do unless faced with the reality of losing a spouse. It took me a while to get over the feeling I was being judged for my life choice, that I must be weaker for making the choice to remarry. I had to let that go, to truly enjoy this new phase of my life. And I did. I am so fortunate to have found love again with an understanding and supportive man.

One of the most unhelpful comments made during that time was, "Well, you can replace your husband, but your kids can't replace their dad." *What?* To people who made that comment, I did not try to explain to them that Jeff and I had been married to our first spouses for a total of 67 years. No one was trying to replace anyone.

I didn't blame my adult children for their initial reactions to my dating Jeff.

Their loss was completely different from mine. It's never time to lose a parent, no matter how old you are. To them it felt too soon for their mother to be dating someone new. I knew I needed to be gentle in my expressions of my need to move forward after grieving. I also understood they were worried about me making an unwise decision, so soon after losing my husband, their father. They slowly accepted the idea of my dating, and Jeff being part of my life.

One of the first times I felt my middle daughter had moved to that spot of acceptance was when she phoned me and when I answered, she said, "Is Jeff there? I need to ask him something." I don't remember the exact question (it was something about a house she and her husband were considering buying), but I do remember the surprised look on Jeff's face when I told him that Shauna needed to talk to him.

Another moment when I felt there was some acceptance of my decision to date was when my oldest Nicole was relating to me a story about her friend's mother-in-law who had been widowed for seventeen years and was really ready to start dating, but didn't know how to move to that phase after being alone for so long. Nicole reported to me that she said to her friend, "She should talk to my mom!"

I think a sudden loss, as several in our group had experienced, did not give any time at all to grieve ahead of time, and that definitely makes the idea of dating again repugnant at first. I did not tell the WGW for many months that I was dating. They suspected something, but waited until I made a 411 call, and they had a lot of questions as I was the first to venture into that territory.

When I started to date Jeff, I told very few people, knowing many would not understand. In fact, I was so torn when Jeff asked me to go to dinner with him I could hardly breathe for a few days. I felt guilty, yet I knew I was not being unfaithful to Terry. I called my friend Diane as she had been so supportive of me during Terry's illness. I felt I could trust her not to be judgmental. I told her of Jeff's invitation, and she immediately said, "You should go." I expressed my feelings of doubt, and she replied, "And I think you should wear that red blouse you were wearing last week." This astounded me. It was okay to go on a date.

I didn't tell my children for a long time, as I knew how hard it would be for them. I wanted to move forward with my life, but I understood their initial reluctance to see that happen so soon.

On one of our early dates, Jeff and I went to a Denver Nuggets basketball game. In the concourse before we went to our seats, Bob, a dear friend from the Denver Hospice support group, was with a group of friends, and came up to me. He hugged me, I introduced him to Jeff, and we went to our seats. During halftime Jeff got up to get us some drinks, and lo and behold, Bob came to my seat. He sat in Jeff's seat, put his arm around me and expressed how happy he was that I was on a date. When Jeff came back to his seat with our drinks, he saw Bob sitting there with his arm around me, making no move to get up. Jeff was nonplussed and simply stood there and talked to us. My worlds were intersecting. A sense of warmth, the security of trusted friendship, flowed through me as I watched these two special men in my life interacting in such a comfortable way.

Bob later told me that seeing me with Jeff gave him the courage to do some online searching, and he eventually met a beautiful, delightful woman whom he married a few years later. In fact, the WGW treated him to his own bachelor party at a happy hour. He posted on Facebook, "You know you are getting old when your bachelor party is with a group of ladies you met at the support group." We were all thrilled to see Bob moving forward.

Dating was one way to move forward, even if there were people who didn't think it was "the right time." We were not replacing anybody, and I won't diminish the awkwardness of dating after decades of marriage, but doing so made me acknowledge my personal need for love and friendship.

Rhonda on dating:

I didn't really date for five years. Briefly, I dated someone after about two years, and I just was not ready. Through various circumstances I started ballroom dancing about five years after Mike passed. That was what brought joy back into my heart. I could do something that was pure enjoyment, and I always felt happy when I left. At that point I was ready to start dating. But the dating world is challenging. Initially, I always compared and no one ever measured up. I've realized it is unfair to do this. I don't feel a need to get married, but would welcome companionship.

Although the kids never vocalized it, I don't think either my kids or Mike's kids would have welcomed someone new into my life in the beginning. They would have outwardly, but inwardly I don't think they wanted me to date. We all had become so close, and this nuclear family couldn't be intruded upon. These last five to six years they have been very open to my dating, even encouraging. Looking back now, I probably grieved too long. I was only 51. Now I am 63 and am now an "older woman." But there is no way to be aware of that in the middle of grieving. It just has to take its course.

Mary on dating:

So many people have success with online dating, so why not give that a try. I started with the Catholic Match app as I am a Catholic and that seemed like a good place to start. I entered all of my qualifications and when I received the notice I was signed up, I was ready to begin searching. I am sure I am not that much of a "catch," but as I scrolled through suggested matches, I was a little disappointed. One that continues to make our group smile was a bio from an elderly gentleman. He too was looking for a companion and stated, "I am really 90 years old, but my friends continue to tell me I do not look a day over 80. I am light on my feet and have most of my teeth." I just had to share this with my new friends and was told to "back away from the computer!" Needless to say, I was not very eager to try any of the other online dating apps.

. 28 .
NEW LIFE, OLD FEAR

WHEN JEFF AND I ATTEND a wedding, there is always a moment during the ceremony where we look at each other sadly and knowingly when the words "till death do us part" are spoken. It strikes us that only one member of the couple will have to deal with that sad reality. It's a good thing, during those happy, idealistic moments that one does not normally think of the possibility that one will be left behind.

I confess it crossed my mind during our wedding ceremony. When Father Don had us repeat those words, they took on a different meaning from when I was a young twenty-one-year-old bride, never imagining that such a day would come. I would never say that to anyone at the time, but I know Jeff probably thought about it on some level as well.

Recently Jeff and I took a road trip to the Grand Canyon. We had a wonderful trip, marveling at the sights of this splendid and incredible national park. We took a lot of pictures of each other and of us together during the week that we were alone there. I was so thrilled to finally visit this site with Jeff. Why then, when we were snapping photos, did the random thought come to my mind that, someday, one of us would be looking at these photos *alone*, remembering a special time in our marriage? The answer is that you simply cannot prevent these thoughts from entering your head, but you now know that the solution is to be in the moment and be grateful for the time you have together. We should always be that way, of course, but the expression "being in the moment" takes on a special meaning when you have experienced that final moment.

Fortunately, our emotional flexibility gave each of us the gift of being able to move forward courageously and lovingly. I am grateful that Jeff chose the song, "Morning Has Broken," as the final song at our wedding, with the congregation singing along. What an apt lyric for a couple forging ahead with life and being appreciative of the gift of resilience.

> *Morning has broken like the first morning*
> *Blackbird has spoken like the first bird*
> *Praise for the singing, praise for the morning*
> *Praise for them springing fresh from the world*

We are thankful for every day this new life has given us.

· 29 ·
ALL WILL BE WELL

"That which does not kill us makes us stronger."
FRIEDRICH NIETZSCHE

IT IS SO HELPFUL being in a group like the WGW. Only the people who have gone through this experience are truly able to understand your pain.

As I was writing this book I received a text from one of the WGW.

Mary wrote:

So! Dan's 1992 truck has been sitting for most of the time since his death. We used it to take my old cabinets to the dump recently but for the most part it sits. It needed some work. Insurance and tags were due so I told the boys to sell it. It sold pretty quickly, and I met the nice young man who bought it. However, I have been weepy all day. Knowing how difficult March is for you I had to reach out and tell you about this. I really didn't see this coming.

Like Mary says, "Even after eleven years, these kinds of things still stop us in our tracks."

Quite often, people will compare being widowed to the experience of getting divorced. While there are certainly similarities—a new reality, your daily life changing around you, having to deal alone with issues, a profound sense of loss—it is not the same. Being with a group of women who went through the experience of the loss of a spouse did more for my healing than anything else I did. Reading books on healing and writing about it were helpful, certainly, but sitting with this group and crying and laughing until my stomach hurt helped heal me like nothing else. To me, there was no substitute for talking it out, crying it out and then laughing with uncensored hilarity at our own black humor.

We dissolved into fits of laughter talking about the monthly newsletter from the Denver Hospice Grief Center with the article entitled, "You're Not Crazy" when Mary said softly, "I didn't receive that one." We railed at the unfairness of life and at our dead spouses for leaving us. We laughed hysterically when someone described her first postmortem sexual experience. We did not need the world to tell us it was okay to grieve together. We had each other. We were forced by death to now be alone. But our unity as the WGW sweetened our lives.

I knew we were getting better when slowly the group would talk about how this grief and loss was a part of life when you have truly loved, and how lucky we were to have loved like that. Eventually, the 911 calls became fewer and fewer as we no longer had to make emergency calls about a fresh stab of grief that we needed to talk out.

As our lives started to fill up again, we acknowledged how proud we were that we could now have a new purpose and meaning to life without feeling guilty. We were now able to adjust to new role changes; for some a new spouse, or other relationship; for Jan, a brand-new snazzy loft apartment in a swanky downtown location that afforded all kinds of opportunities to get out and about; for Karen, the race car driving that she took up; for others, travel to exotic places on our readjusted bucket lists. We were now able to acknowledge that we have discovered new parts of ourselves that would never have emerged without this shared experience. We did not "get over" our grief. We just found new ways of moving forward and having new purpose and meaning in our new reality.

This is not to say I don't still sometimes fall to pieces when I hear Bob Seger's song, "Against the Wind," or that I don't feel a twinge when I look at the calendar and see that March is approaching. But I am no longer preoccupied with thoughts of Terry. There is a new sense of release from having to think about him constantly. I can say that after two years or so, most of the WGW felt this new release and were able to now live life and enjoy it without any feelings of guilt or shame.

We still have our monthly dinners and happy hours, but there is no urgency anymore, we are simply together as a group that knew and supported each other at the rawest and most vulnerable times of our lives. We had given each other a precious gift: the freedom to laugh, cry, rail, weep, mourn, and then laugh, and dance.

I like this line from Garth Brooks' song, "The Dance." It captures perfectly what we all acknowledged: Recovering from this experience made us grateful that we had the love in our lives that, when losing it, still made us grateful that we had it.

> *And now I'm glad I didn't know*
> *The way it all would end, the way it all would go*
> *Our lives are better left to chance*
> *I could have missed the pain*
> *But I'd have had to miss the dance*
> Garth Brooks: "The Dance"

Things will never be the same, but we are grateful for the new reality, meaning, and purpose in life.

We started this journey as heartbroken souls, hardly able to get out of bed in the morning, much less productive, but became strong resilient women who made a new place for ourselves in life, moving forward with confidence and gratefulness. We found ourselves capable of so much more than we had ever imagined we could be.

We no longer need each other for the same depth of support we needed at the beginning, but we now enjoy this strong friendship—born out of grief and sadness—that has become one of resilience.

Resilience. I love that word. It makes me feel so strong.

For a long, long time I still had a wistful longing for what I had lost, and it returns occasionally to this day, when I then remind myself, "Look how far you have come." George Bonanno, author of *The Other Side of Sadness* focuses on the natural resilience of bereaved people. When my sister Karen gave me his book, she said,

"This book reminds me of you." Most bereaved people, in fact, are not destroyed by their grief. Our old ideas of grief and mourning tell us we have to go through certain "stages" and they must be done "in sequence" to be fully recovered. The truth is you never fully recover in the ways you would like to be, but one day, you wake up surprised by a sense of calm and know that all will be well.

ACKNOWLEDGEMENTS

I gratefully acknowledge:
Debbie, Mary, Janet, Jan, Karen, Rhonda, and Sue: the Widows Gone Wild. Without your support, encouragement, humor, and love, the *Club That Nobody Wants to Join* would have been a much lonelier place.

My children Nicole, Shauna, and Joel, and your spouses Dan and Ellen. I am grateful for your presence in my life as we all went through our difficult loss. Also, to my grandchildren Alyssa, Emma, Audrey, Michael, Matthew, Hannah, Iris, Viola, and Adam. You will never know the depth of my gratitude for keeping me laughing and loving through these past years. Grandpa Terry would be so proud of you.

My husband, Jeff, for his encouragement and thoughtful feedback with this book, and for just loving me. May we have many more years together.

My siblings, who helped me navigate the difficult days after Terry's death with encouragement and support, and who supported me in the writing of this memoir.

My close friends, too numerous to mention, who said and did

the right things to keep me on the road to hope. I am forever grateful for your unrelenting support and love.

The Denver Hospice, for the wonderful experience I had with the Younger Bereaved Spouses support group. I can honestly say I would not be the same resilient person without your wonderful counselors, your newsletters, and your gentle guidance.

My editor, Kathy Groom, for your assurance that there was really a book in me, and for your corrections, humor, and knowledge throughout this process. I truly think we were meant to meet and work together.

REFERENCES

Guideline content courtesy of The Denver Hospice, Denver, CO, 2019

Elizabeth Kubler-Ross and David Kessler, *On Grief and Grieving: Finding the Meaning of Grief Through The Five Stages of Loss,* (Scribner House, 2005)

Joan Didion, *The Year of Magical Thinking*, (HighBridge Company, 2005)

Elizabeth Berg, *The Dream Lover*, (Penguin Random House, 2016)

George A. Bonanno, *The Other Side of Sadness: What the Science of Bereavement Tells Us About Life After Loss*, (Basic Books, 2009)

Joan D. Chittister, *The Gift of Years: Growing Older Gracefully*, (BlueBridge, 2008)

Pat Schweibert, Chuck DeKlyen, and Taylor Mills, *Tear Soup: A Recipe for Healing After Loss*, Grief Watch, 2005)

Mary Oliver, "The Summer Day," from *House of Light*, (Beacon Press, 1990)

John Pavlovitz, "The Mourning After: Grieving Someone We Love," (from the digital collection: Johnpavlovitz.com, 2017)

Nietsche, Frederich, *Twilight of the Idols*, 1889

Campbell, Joseph, "Reflections on the Art of Living: A Joseph Campbell Companion," Selected and edited by Diane K. Osbon, (New York: HarperCollins, 1991) Quote Page 8 and 18

"You Can Close Your Eyes," James Taylor, from the album Mud Slide Slim and The Blue Horizon, 1991

"Against the Wind," Bob Seger, 1980

"The Dance," Garth Brooks, Written by Tony Arata, 1990

"Jack and Diane," John Mellencamp, 1982

"Morning Has Broken," Eleanor Farjeon, tune BunessonG, 1931

ABOUT THE AUTHOR

Sunny Wells is a retired French teacher, writer, and speaker who offers hope to young bereaved widows. Besides joining her Widows Gone Wild friends on continued adventures, Sunny and her new husband split their time between their homes in Colorado and Florida. They love to travel and to spend time with their 11 grandchildren. Her website is widowsgonewildthebook.com.

www.ingramcontent.com/pod-product-compliance
Lightning Source LLC
Chambersburg PA
CBHW020417080526
44584CB00014B/1376